FAMILY MEALS

MICHAEL SMITH
FAMILY MEALS

Photography by Ryan Szulc

PENGUIN

an imprint of Penguin Canada Books Inc., a Penguin Random House Company

Published by the Penguin Group

Penguin Canada Books Inc., 90 Eglinton Avenue East, Suite 700, Toronto, Ontario, Canada M4P 2Y3

Penguin Group (USA) LLC, 375 Hudson Street, New York, New York 10014, U.S.A.

Penguin Books Ltd, 80 Strand, London WC2R 0RL, England

Penguin Ireland, 25 St Stephen's Green, Dublin 2, Ireland (a division of Penguin Books Ltd)

Penguin Group (Australia), 707 Collins Street, Melbourne, Victoria 3008, Australia (a division of
        Pearson Australia Group Pty Ltd)

Penguin Books India Pvt Ltd, 11 Community Centre, Panchsheel Park, New Delhi – 110 017, India

Penguin Group (NZ), 67 Apollo Drive, Rosedale, Auckland 0632, New Zealand (a division of Pearson
        New Zealand Ltd)

Penguin Books (South Africa) (Pty) Ltd, 24 Sturdee Avenue, Rosebank, Johannesburg 2196,
        South Africa

Penguin Books Ltd, Registered Offices: 80 Strand, London WC2R 0RL, England

First published 2014

1 2 3 4 5 6 7 8 9 10 (CR)

Food photography by Ryan Szulc
Food styling by Noah Witenoff
Prop styling by Madeleine Johari

Photo on page 58 by Gabe Smith

Manufactured in the U.S.A.

Library and Archives Canada Cataloguing in Publication

Smith, Michael, author
        Family meals / Michael Smith.

Includes index.
        ISBN 978-0-14-318411-9 (pbk.)

1. Quick and easy cooking. 2. Cookbooks. I. Title.

TX833.5.S649 2014   641.5'55   C2014-901285-3

eBook ISBN 978-0-14-319294-7

Visit the Penguin Canada website at **www.penguin.ca**

Special and corporate bulk purchase rates available; please see **www.penguin.ca/corporatesales**
        or call 1-800-810-3104.

This book is dedicated to the true heroes of food: the family cooks. Every day we face the greatest challenges in the world of cooking, and every time we cook, we earn the best reward!

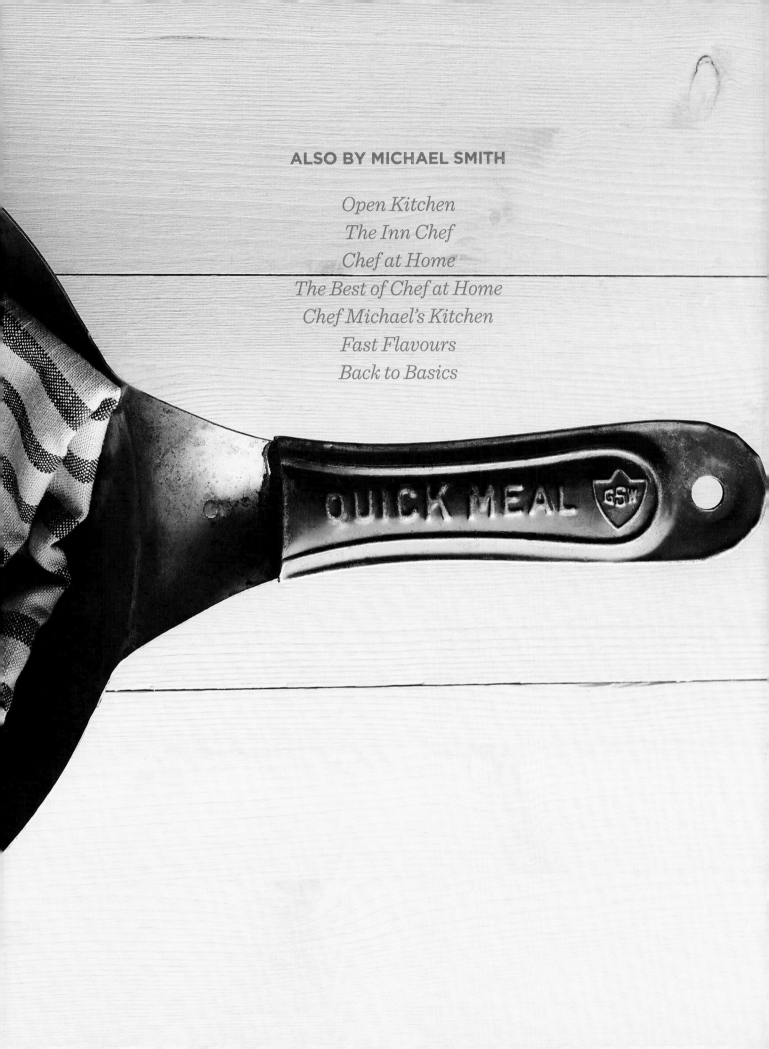

ALSO BY MICHAEL SMITH

Open Kitchen
The Inn Chef
Chef at Home
The Best of Chef at Home
Chef Michael's Kitchen
Fast Flavours
Back to Basics

CONTENTS

COOK REAL FOOD FOR YOUR FAMILY

I'M PROUD OF ALL THAT I'VE ACHIEVED AS A PROFESSIONAL CHEF. I'VE apprenticed in Europe, run top-ten restaurants, cooked at two Olympics, traveled to thirty countries searching for flavors, written seven (now eight) cookbooks, hosted five cooking shows and much, much more. But all those achievements pale in comparison to that magical moment when one of my kids takes their first bite of dinner, smiles and digs in for more.

I may be a busy guy (and who isn't these days?) but I cook every single day for my family. Day after day after day. It's always rewarding, often inspiring and occasionally a chore. But it's never optional. We lead busy lives but we have to eat, and processed food is simply not an option for my family. It doesn't need to be one for yours either.

But in between hockey practice, gymnastics lessons, music lessons, play rehearsals, supervising homework, work projects, appointments, lawn mowing and snow shoveling, finding the time to cook real food for your family is a challenge. No one knows that more than I do.

This book shares the hard-earned lessons I've learned on the front lines in my own home, doing what I do best for my beautiful wife, three kids, two dogs and one cat. Here are lots of simple ideas and easy dishes that anyone can prepare with ingredients that you can find at your supermarket and tools you already have. Most important, this book is packed with reality and insight—from one family cook to another.

Cooking for your family can be one of the most rewarding things you can do in your life. And real food is the right way to go. The decisions you make in your kitchen now will have profound effects in the years ahead. We truly are what we eat, and none of us wants to be factory-made. Homemade all the way!

My best advice? Relax. It's just food. Humans have cooked for millions of years, and you can too. Don't confuse the unfamiliar with difficult. And remember: we're not striving for perfection. Leave that stress to the professional chefs. We're family cooks just trying to get real food on the table.

Now if I can just find the time to tackle that pile of dishes and remember to take the garbage out before the truck comes.

FAMILY COOKING

10 WAYS TO COOK TOGETHER

1. **FIRST AND FOREMOST, DECIDE THAT COOKING IS FUN, NOT WORK.** Gathering, preparing and sharing, every step is rewarding. Don't worry about the mess, throw caution to the wind and just dive in. And the more your family shares the fun, the better!

2. **BEGIN BY SHOPPING TOGETHER.** Take your kids along when you can and involve them. Focus on fresh produce by encouraging them to pick a few things out: sweet ripe fruit, one of their favorite vegetables and something new and unknown. Adopt them. Cook them. Enjoy them!

3. **GO BEYOND THE FARMERS' MARKET AND MEET A FARMER.** Support local so your kids can meet and get to know real people making real food. Teach them that food is personal and special.

4. **CREATE A FOOD BUDGET.** Use it to teach your family many, many money lessons. Help your kids apply classroom math to the real world as they figure out how much dinner or a week's food costs.

5. **COOK TOGETHER.** Figure out how to share and get along in the kitchen and how to celebrate food and make it fun for all. Find your family's path through the kitchen and explore it together.

6. **USE COOKIE SHEETS AS SMALL WORK STATIONS.** These are great to organize recipe ingredients and contain any mess. Try not to worry about speed; it comes with time. Slow and steady progress through a dish always works.

7. **APPOINT FAMILY EXPERTS TO MASTER CERTAIN STANDARD TASKS.** In my house all egg-cracking is handled by my daughter and all nutmeg grating by her brother. They're proud of their skills and thrilled when they're called to action. They set the table too, but that's an everyday task, more like a chore and that's another story!

8. **SET UP AN OUTDOOR GRILL OR BARBECUE AND COOK ON IT AS MUCH AS POSSIBLE.** Not only is it easy and tasty, but it's always an occasion. Cooking outside makes food seem special. Do it as long as you can while the weather is good and while the grill is hot throw on a prep job or two. Try grilling some vegetables or meat for further dishes. Thick eggplant slices, slabs of red onion and halved zucchinis are all a revelation on the grill.

9. **EAT TOGETHER.** Find the time, make it happen and enjoy your meals together. Close the loop and share the food and the time together. It's the whole point of cooking, to come together as a family and share. Let your food choices honor the occasion.

10. **POP REAL POPCORN.** Of all the fun things you can do in a kitchen with your kids, perhaps none is as exciting as popping corn the old-fashioned way. Use a pot and let it fly. The drama is irresistible. A lid will eventually contain the treat but by then the memories will have been made!

NEED MORE RECIPE IDEAS FOR COOKING TOGETHER? TRY THESE:

WEEKDAY TIPS

10 WAYS TO KEEP YOUR FAMILY KITCHEN RUNNING SMOOTHLY

1. **PLAN AHEAD.** My number one piece of advice is spend time to save time. On the weekend, create a weekly planning routine that works for you, then organize the meals, shopping, preparation, cooking and cleaning. Share the tasks and assign jobs to family members if you can. Planning ahead for a busy week is definitely time well spent!

2. **COOK AHEAD.** Seize every chance you get to do two things at once. I often brown beef stewing cuts and set them to simmering with a bottle of full-bodied red wine for tomorrow while cooking something else tonight.

3. **WEEKEND PREP.** Try to fit in some cooking time. Fill your slow cooker. Prep another dish. Set a timer for one hour and get everyone in on the act of slicing, dicing and prepping for the week ahead. Make some cookies or brownies. Bake with your family. Make some memories!

4. **ASSIGN MEALS.** As your kids get older they can join the adults and take on cooking dinner one night of the week. Engage them with the details, let them show off a favorite dish or try something new. Someday they'll thank you. Maybe even today.

5. **DOUBLE UP.** Always make more than you need because in the long run you'll always save time. Take pancakes, for instance. Today's batter is perfect for tomorrow's waffles—one bowl, two different breakfasts. In my house that usually means Sunday pancakes, then Monday waffles, our favourite weekend ritual and a fun send-off for the school week.

6. **BREAKFAST FOR DINNER.** The hearty flavors of breakfast are right at home on the dinner table. Homemade pancakes, fluffy waffles, thick French toast, bacon and eggs, omelets and frittatas all look great next to a balanced light green salad.

7. **FAMILY STYLE TABLE.** Try sharing and serving meals "family style" on platters or in bowls. It's easier for the cook and simple to set up the table. Everyone can serve themselves—a perfect way to please different appetites. And, as always, leftovers are tomorrow's lunch just waiting to happen.

8. **EASY CHICKEN BROTH.** Always gather the remains, the bones and scraps of a roast chicken dinner. They're another meal waiting to happen. Just toss in some onion, carrot, celery and a bay leaf, cover with water and a lid, simmer slowly, stirring occasionally, and in just two hours you'll have rich broth poised for another meal like my Asian Chicken Noodle Soup, page 111, and Pizza Soup, page 116. Homemade chicken broth ready-to-go in the refrigerator is a great weekday time saver.

9. **BABY FOOD.** It's all about the texture. You can take the dinner pushed aside last night, mash it, even purée it, jar and freeze the works and it'll pass with flying colors the next day!

10. **ORGANIZE A NEIGHBORHOOD BAKING RALLY.** Create a baking club and get everyone trading weekly muffins, treats, breads, loaves, ideas and spirit.

NEED MORE WEEKDAY RECIPE IDEAS? TRY THESE:

TIDY TIPS

10 STRATEGIES FOR ORGANIZING YOUR FAMILY KITCHEN

1. **GROCERY LIST.** A well-crafted, diligently used grocery list is a thing of beauty and an essential tool for any kitchen. Keep one going and continuously updated so you're always ready to cook! You can download mine at chefmichaelsmith.com and customize it for your family.

2. **PLAN THE MESS.** Before you start cooking consider the discard ahead and be ready for it. Position a scrap bowl on the counter and use it as you work. Have an array of task bowls and pans ready to receive your prep and keep your work surface organized.

3. **DISHWASHER CLEAN.** When prepping, try not to pile raw food on your countertops or work surfaces; it can be very unhygienic. Instead, hold the variously prepped foods on clean plates or prep bowls scrubbed clean and sanitized in your dishwasher.

4. **CLEAN AS YOU GO.** My long, storied career in the kitchens of the world has more than proven to me that taking the time to clean as you go always saves you time in the end. It teaches discipline too and that's not a bad thing either!

5. **BRIBE YOUR KIDS.** Legions of parents attach scullery duties to weekly allowances. Why shouldn't you? You should! This is one of the only socially acceptable forms of child labour, so milk it. Teach them craftsmanship, set a high standard, and trust but verify, then offer a small stipend for their services in the form of a weekly allowance. Who knows? This might motivate your kids to learn to cook, and then they won't have to clean up!

6. **RECRUIT HELP.** The whole point of having guests for supper is to spread the love and the labor. So be bold, seize the moment and arm yourself with a crack team to ease the pain of the postprandial dish pit.

7. **OVEN LINERS.** Whenever you put a pan or dish in your oven, consider placing it on a shallow baking tray to contain any food that bubbles over. Protect the hard-fought cleanliness of your oven bottom. It's much easier than scraping away incinerated carbon.

8. **CARE FOR YOUR TOOLS.** Good cooks take particular care of their pots and knives. Scrub them clean inside and out, each and every time, never allowing the residue of one job to overlap the next.

9. **BURNT SUGAR.** Don't let small problems become big ones. Clean up baking messes as you go. In a pinch any pot or pan surface blackened with any form of sugar should be soaked in water. The sugar will dissolve with time. Sometimes quickly, sometimes slower.

10. **THE KIDS' DRAWER.** Every kitchen is a magnet for kids and their stuff. If you want to give yourself a slim chance at containing the mess, it's best to have a low drawer waiting for it. See how fast your kids can fill it when it's time to clean up and you dangle a treat!

BREAKFAST & BRUNCH

FAMILY RECIPES

A GOOD-MORNING WAKE-UP FOR THE MIND, BODY AND SOUL, THIS GRANOLA RECIPE perfectly kicks off *Family Meals*. It's real old-fashioned granola with great flavor that, hands down, beats anything from the store. Build your own from this basic method, then customize it any way you want. It's ridiculously easy and deliciously nutritious. MAKES 20 CUPS (5 L) OR SO

NUTTY SEEDY GRANOLA

THE BASE INGREDIENTS

1 cup (250 mL) of any vegetable oil

1 cup (250 mL) of honey

1 tablespoon (15 mL) or so of cinnamon

1 tablespoon (15 mL) or so of nutmeg

1 tablespoon (15 mL) of pure
vanilla extract

8 cups (2 L) of oats (instant, large-flake
or steel-cut)

CUSTOM INGREDIENTS

3 cups (750 mL) of any nuts (such
as almonds, walnuts, pecans,
hazelnuts, macadamia, peanuts, pine
nuts, cashews)

3 cups (750 mL) of any seeds (such
as chia, flax, sunflower, pumpkin,
hemp hearts)

2 cups (500 mL) of any dried fruit
(such as raisins, cherries, apricots,
figs, dates, even those little sugar-
bomb dried cranberries)

Preheat your oven to 325°F (160°C). Line 2 baking sheets with parchment paper or foil and lightly oil the paper or foil.

Measure the oil into a small saucepan. Use the same measuring cup for the honey (to avoid the sticky mess); add the honey to the oil along with the cinnamon, nutmeg and vanilla. Whisk until smooth and thin. Heat over medium heat, whisking occasionally, until the honey has melted into the oil.

Toss the oats into a large bowl, then pour the spiced honey over them. Stir until everything is thoroughly and evenly combined. Divide the mixture between the baking sheets, spreading to an even layer. (Set the bowl aside.) Bake, stirring every 10 minutes or so to ensure even browning, for about 40 minutes or until the granola is golden brown and fragrant.

Combine your chosen nuts, seeds and dried fruits in the bowl. If any of the pieces are too large for your spoon, cut them down to size. Carefully scrape the hot granola into the bowl, then toss the works together. Set aside to cool. Transfer to an airtight container or a resealable plastic bag. This granola stays fresh for up to a week (as if it will last that long ...).

FAMILY FLAVORS

There are so many nuts, seeds and dried fruits to choose from that this recipe is a perfect canvas for personal expression. Experiment and find your own family's favorite. Kids can create their own custom blends for their personal stash or as the Flavor-of-the-Week for all. Make a big batch on the weekend and guarantee a powerful start to every day for your family.

This granola is great with yogurt for breakfast, lunch or an after school snack. It's even better in a parfait with layers of your favorite fruit added.

FAMILY FLAVORS

Every family needs a good blender, and as long as you fill yours with fruity smoothies, you'll be fine. But it's just as fine to put an easy evening spin on things now and again. Drop the yogurt in favor of a couple handfuls of ice. Voilà—the family blender strikes again!

BPA FREE

LTRS
MAX
1.4
1.2
1.0
0.8
0.6
0.4
0.2

CUPS
6
5
4
3
2
1

EY, DAD, HOCK THE TOOL KIT AND OUTSOURCE THE LAWN MOWER. WHAT YOU really need is a high-speed blender so you can add this morning power boost to your family's weekday routine. With your new toy, you can easily create a brand-new batch of smoothie love every day of the week. And when the kids aren't around, a boozy slushie is just as easy as a fruity smoothie. SERVES 4

FAMILY SMOOTHIES

Loosely fill your blender with your chosen ingredients, measuring with abandon and throwing culinary caution to the winds. If by chance it's after 5 p.m., consider opening the bar. Either way, purée vigorously. Have a taste, close your eyes and make up a memorable name. Sell the sizzle! Serve and share!

REAL SIMPLE SMOOTHIE

½ bag (8 to 10 ounces/225 to 280 g) of fiber-filled frozen fruit

2 or 3 fresh bananas

3 to 4 cups (750 mL to 1 L) of carb-loaded orange juice

2 cups (500 mL) of protein-rich yogurt

2 spoonfuls of energy-packed honey

2 spoonfuls of nutritionally dense flaxseed oil

Aromatic herbs, spices and various friendly flavors

SMOOTHIE VARIATIONS

STRAWBERRY MINT

4 cups (1 L) of frozen strawberries

4 cups (1 L) of orange juice

2 cups (500 mL) of strawberry yogurt

2 tablespoons (30 mL) or so of honey

1 bunch of fresh mint (leaves and soft stems)

SPICE ISLAND BANANA

4 soft ripe bananas

4 cups (1 L) of orange juice

2 cups (500 mL) of vanilla-flavored yogurt

2 tablespoons (30 mL) of honey

1 teaspoon (5 mL) of nutmeg

1 teaspoon (5 mL) of pure vanilla extract

TROPICAL FRUIT

4 cups (1 L) of frozen mango or tropical fruit mix

2 cups (500 mL) of pineapple or orange juice

2 cups (250 mL) of plain yogurt

1 can (14 ounces/400 mL) of coconut milk

2 tablespoons (30 mL) or so of honey

The zest and juice of 1 lime

NEED A FAST GRAB-AND-GO BREAKFAST FOR THE WHOLE FAMILY THAT'S TASTY, nutritious and on-the-fly? Look no further than the old stir-and-store trick. It's a bit offbeat, but it works: soaking the oatmeal in milk overnight makes it tender. Before you crash for the night, mix up tomorrow's breakfast jars of goodness, then wake up to a morning jolt of flavor, nutrition and family fuel. These breakfast jars are equally impressive when slowly enjoyed on weekends. MAKES FOUR 1-PINT (500 ML) MASON JARS, SERVES 4

OVERNIGHT OATMEAL JARS WITH LAST-MINUTE STIR-INS

FOR THE P.M. BASE

4 cups (1 L) of quick-cooking
  or large-flake rolled oats

4 tablespoons (60 mL) of maple syrup,
  brown sugar or honey

1 teaspoon (5 mL) of cinnamon
  or your favorite baking spice

1 teaspoon (5 mL) of pure
  vanilla extract

½ teaspoon (2 mL) of salt

4 cups (1 L) of any milk (dairy, soy,
  rice or nut)

2 cups (500 mL) of your favorite frozen
  fruit (berries, tropical or tree)

FOR THE A.M. TOPPING

2 cups (500 mL) of your favorite
  yogurt (optional)

¼ to ½ cup (60 to 125 mL) of maple
  syrup, brown sugar or honey

1 cup (250 mL) of crispy crunchy nuts
  or seeds

Measure the oats, syrup, cinnamon, vanilla, salt and milk evenly into four 1-pint (500 mL) mason jars. Seal the jars and give the works a good shake. Top with a thick layer of frozen fruit. Chill overnight (or even for 2 nights).

In the morning, top off the smoothly transformed oatmeal with yogurt (if desired), a splash of sweet syrup and your crunch of choice. If dashing out the door with breakfast, don't forget to grab a spoon!

FAMILY FLAVORS

There's no shame in rushing into your day, but it's a lot easier when you're fortified with flavorful fuel. You can make a lot of these jars in advance and they're fun for your kids to personalize every morning with their choice of fruit and yogurt.

WHO SAYS COOKING HAS TO BE COMPLICATED? FRY SOME BACON, WHISK SOME eggs and Cheddar together, fry the works in the hot bacon fat and slip it into a speedy sandwich. Nothing beats a handmade kick start any day of the week. MAKES ENOUGH FOR AN A.M. FEED FOR 1 OR 2, EASILY SHARED, EASILY DOUBLED

EVERY-DAY EGG SANDWICH

Slap the bacon into your favorite small nonstick skillet. Turn the heat to medium-high and start listening. A simmering pan means nothing. Sizzle is the sound of flavor. Too loud, though, and a sizzling pan quickly becomes a smoking-burning pan. After 10 minutes or so, when the bacon is browned and crispy, turn down the heat and pour off half the fat.

Meanwhile, start the coffee, then crack the eggs into a bowl and add the cheese, herb and pepper. Whisk vigorously. Pour over the bacon and stir briefly, just enough to combine evenly. Fry, without stirring, just until the eggy, bacony goodness is lightly browned on the bottom and firm enough to flip, then deftly turn over the works with a spatula. Fry until the eggs are cooked through, another couple of minutes. Tuck between slices of toast, and serve and share!

2, 3 or even 4 slices of bacon, stacked and thinly sliced
2 or 3 eggs
1 to 2 ounces (28 to 55 g) of shredded Cheddar cheese
A handful of chopped fresh thyme, parsley or green onions
A few turns of your pepper grinder
Awesome artisanal bread, for toasting

FAMILY FLAVORS

You can customize these eggs in a million different ways, so if you have another idea, go for it! The point is to make breakfast for your family and not let some factory do it. I really like my sandwich with sliced juicy tomatoes.

THESE PANCAKES ARE FOR SHARING, EVERY STEP OF THE WAY: FLOUR MEASURING, egg cracking, expensive vanilla spilling, flour volcanoes, vigorous spooning and fearless flipping. My kids will never forget all the good times we've had making these pancakes, and I'll remember forever how healthy they were every single time. Try them—you'll remember how much fun it is to cook with your family.

SERVES 4 TO 6, EASILY DOUBLED

WEEKEND PANCAKES

KID 1: THE DRY INGREDIENTS

1 cup (250 mL) of unbleached all-
   purpose flour
1 cup (250 mL) of whole wheat flour
1 cup (250 mL) of quick-cooking
   rolled oats
2 tablespoons (30 mL) of
   baking powder
1 teaspoon (5 mL) of cinnamon
   or nutmeg
½ teaspoon (2 mL) of salt

KID 2 OR PARENT: THE WET INGREDIENTS

2 expertly cracked eggs
2 cups (500 mL) of any milk (dairy
   or otherwise)
2 tablespoons (30 mL) of vegetable
   oil or melted butter, plus more for
   the pan
2 tablespoons (30 mL) of honey
1 tablespoon (15 mL) of pure
   vanilla extract

While the kids get out bowls and measure the wet and dry ingredients, heat your largest, heaviest skillet or griddle over medium-high heat. Gas, electric, induction or campfire—strive for that magical mark just past halfway, where food sizzles and browns without burning.

Share the whisk so you don't have to wash two of them. First whisk the dry ingredients together, then give the wet team a turn. Switch to a wooden spoon and gradually stir the wet into the dry, letting everybody stir the works a bit and not worrying whether the batter will be mixed wrong. Just make sure the batter is evenly combined.

Coat your hot pan with a swirl of vegetable oil. Spoon in the batter, filling the pan with any size or shape of pancakes. Cook until the bottom of every last pancake is golden brown before flamboyantly flipping the flapjacks. Continue cooking for a few minutes longer until the pancakes are firm. If need be, keep warm in a 200°F (100°C) oven while you repeat with the remaining batter, dealing pancakes like you're working the Vegas strip. Devour with lots of decadently melting butter and of course a long pour of real maple syrup—none of that Auntie-artificial corn syrup stuff for these high-grade pancakes! Serve and share!

FAMILY FLAVORS

Cooking together is fun for every family and can even become a tradition. Pancakes are the perfect place to start. Build anticipation. Days in advance. Whispered rumors, good-night promises, that sort of thing. In the morning rally your team in the kitchen. Share the prep, build the batter, man the pans and do the divvy.

NOTHING BEATS A FRESH GOLDEN WAFFLE FOR BREAKFAST. HERE, A RIPE BANANA smoothly transforms rich butter into an inspired topping. It's easy to stir together homemade waffle batter and fill it with rich butter and buttermilk, but it's the aromatic nutmeg that makes these breakfast treats memorable. This Caribbean spice is famously delicious and mysteriously exotic. SERVES 4 TO 6

NUTMEG WAFFLES WITH BANANA BUTTER

Preheat your waffle iron.

Craft the banana butter by simply mashing the soft banana with the soft butter, floral honey and aromatic vanilla until combined, making it as smooth as you like. (A food processor delivers super smoothness.)

For the waffles, in a large bowl, whisk together the flour, baking powder, baking soda, nutmeg and salt. In a medium bowl, whisk together the eggs, buttermilk and butter. Pour the wet over the dry and stir the works until the batter is smooth and even.

Lightly spray the waffle iron with cooking spray. Spoon enough batter into the center to cover half of the cooking surface, thus leaving lots of room for expansion. Close the lid and cook until the waffles are crisp and golden brown, 5 minutes or so. Keep an eye on the steam: it'll just about stop when the waffles are ready. If you feel any resistance as you lift the lid, give the waffle another minute. If need be, keep warm in a 200°F (100°C) oven while you repeat with the remaining batter. Serve and share with big dollops of the banana butter!

FOR THE BANANA BUTTER

1 ripe banana
¼ cup (60 mL) of butter, at room temperature
1 tablespoon (15 mL) of honey
¼ teaspoon (1 mL) of pure vanilla extract

FOR THE WAFFLES

3 cups (750 mL) of all-purpose flour
1 tablespoon (15 mL) of baking powder
1 teaspoon (5 mL) of baking soda
1 teaspoon (5 mL) of nutmeg
½ teaspoon (2 mL) of salt
3 eggs
3 cups (750 mL) of well-shaken buttermilk or regular milk
1 cup (250 mL) of butter, melted and cooled

FAMILY FLAVORS

The sight of the steam-pumping waffle iron chugging away on the kitchen counter may be intimidating at first, but with practice your kids can easily run the waffle works. Safety first, and with time comes trust and ultimately pride in new successes—in life and the kitchen.

LOOKING FOR A BREAKFAST-IN-BED TREAT OR SOMETHING TO MAKE THE WEEKEND special? This is it. For maximum brownie points, make the compote in advance so it has time to cool and thicken. (Or not! It's awesome straight out of the pan too.) Stumble into the kitchen, crack a few eggs, whisk, dip and fry—and come out looking like a hero. SERVES 4, WITH LEFTOVER DELICIOUS COMPOTE

FRENCH TOAST WITH STRAWBERRY GINGER COMPOTE

FOR THE STRAWBERRY GINGER COMPOTE

1 cup (250 mL) of strawberry jam

A splash of orange juice

The zest and juice of 1 lemon

2 inches (5 cm) or so of frozen ginger

4 cups (1 L) of frozen strawberries

FOR THE FRENCH TOAST

4 eggs

1 cup (250 mL) of milk

½ cup (125 mL) of brown sugar

1 tablespoon (15 mL) of pure
   vanilla extract

2 teaspoons (10 mL) of cinnamon
   or nutmeg

8 or more thick slices of your favorite
   multigrain bread

2 tablespoons (30 mL) or more
   of vegetable oil

2 tablespoons (30 mL) or more
   of butter

Make the compote ahead of time, even the day before. Spoon the jam into a medium saucepan, splash in the orange juice and stir in the lemon zest and juice. Finely grate the frozen ginger into the works using a microplane grater. Bring to a steady simmer over high heat, then stir in the frozen strawberries. Continue cooking, stirring gently, just long enough to heat through the compote. Pour into a jar or bowl and refrigerate until chilled.

For the French toast, heat your largest, heaviest skillet or griddle over medium-high heat. Gas, electric, induction or campfire—strive for that magical mark just past halfway, where food sizzles and browns without burning.

Crack the eggs into a large bowl and whisk in the milk, brown sugar, vanilla and cinnamon. Add as many bread slices as will fit in your pan at one time, gently turning each slice and letting the bread absorb lots of the flavorful mixture. Your patience here will be rewarded with maximum flavor.

Pour a small puddle of oil into the hot pan, then add the butter and gently swirl until golden brown and sizzling. Immediately add the bread slices. Cook until the bottom is golden brown and crisp, 3 or 4 minutes, then flip and cook a few minutes more. If need be, keep warm in a 200°F (100°C) oven while you repeat with the remaining bread. Divvy, serve and share with heaps of strawberry love!

FAMILY FLAVORS
- - - - - - - - - -
Nothing is more fun for kids than collaborating with one parent to make breakfast in bed for the other parent or a birthday sibling. Occasions like these have a happy way of turning into sacred traditions. And the kids think it's just food!

A ROUND OF SAVORY BREAKFAST BURRITOS IS A GREAT WAY TO DELIVER THE OLD eggs 'n' bacon one-two punch with a brand-new twist. The sunny flavors of the bright Southwest are welcome any time of day but especially shine in this morning staple. These burritos are super easy and deliciously hearty. In my house, we like them so much they've earned the nickname the 5Bs! MAKES 4 BURRITOS

BACON BLACK BEAN BREAKFAST BURRITO

Toss the bacon into a heavy nonstick skillet. Add 1 cup (250 mL) of water (this helps the bacon cook evenly). Set the heat to medium-high and cook, stirring often, until the water is evaporated and the bacon is crisp, 10 minutes or so.

Splash a little more water into the pan and stir to clean up the bottom a bit. Pour in the beans, salsa, cumin and hot sauce. Continue cooking and stirring just long enough for the mixture to heat through. Add the eggs and continue cooking and stirring until they firm up, just 2 or 3 minutes longer.

Ready the tortillas by briefly microwaving them until soft and pliable, 30 seconds or so. Arrange the tortillas on your work surface. Place one-quarter of the filling just below the "equator" of each. Top with a quarter of the cheese and some fresh cilantro. Fold the bottom of the tortilla over the filling, fold in the sides, then finish rolling. Serve and share!

8 slices of bacon, diced

A 19-ounce (540 mL) can of black beans, drained and rinsed

¼ cup (60 mL) of your favorite salsa

1 teaspoon (5 mL) of ground cumin or chili powder

As much of your favorite hot sauce as you like

4 eggs, lightly beaten

4 large soft whole wheat tortillas

1 cup (250 mL) of shredded Cheddar cheese

A handful of fresh cilantro leaves and tender stems

FAMILY FLAVORS

A lot of burrito recipes call for cooking the individual elements—the bacon, the beans, the eggs—separately. That may be a touch more authentic, but you'd need an arsenal of pans and a team of pot washers. In the real world there's a premium on recipes that use just one pan—and use it just once.

EGGS ARE MAGICAL, AND A SIMPLE FRITTATA PACKED WITH FLAVOR IS THE PERFECT place to let them shine. This classic method is an easy way to get a lot of morning flavor on the table in a hurry and maybe even pull your family together for a spontaneous shared meal. SERVES 6, EVEN 8 IN A PINCH

BROCCOLI BACON FRITTATA

8 slices of thick-cut bacon, diced

1 bunch of broccoli, cut into
  small florets

Salt and pepper

12 eggs

½ cup (125 mL) of milk

2 cups (500 mL) of shredded
  Cheddar cheese

FAMILY FLAVORS

It's easy for your family to pass through the kitchen in the morning following separate, barely overlapping routines, grabbing something nutritionally functional yet blandly boring. A dish like this will inspire everyone to stop and share some time together. Be deliberate. Stay present. You'll love this simple classic even more.

Preheat your oven to 350°F (180°C). Turn on your convection fan if you have one.

Toss the bacon into a large, heavy ovenproof nonstick skillet. Add 1 cup (250 mL) of water (this helps the bacon cook evenly). Set the heat to medium-high and cook, stirring often, until the water is evaporated and the bacon is crisp, 10 minutes or so.

Remove the bacon with a slotted spoon, leaving some or all of the delicious fat behind. Reduce the heat to medium and add the broccoli in a single layer. Season it lightly with salt and pepper and add ½ cup (125 mL) of water. Bring to a steady simmer, gently stirring and loosening flavors from the bottom of the pan. Cover and continue cooking until the broccoli is just tender, a minute or two more. Remove the lid and pour off any remaining water.

Whisk together the eggs, milk, cheese and ¼ teaspoon (1 mL) of salt. Pour over the broccoli. Add the bacon. Stir gently as large curds form, until about half the mixture is set, 2 or 3 minutes. Stop stirring so the bottom will brown and form a crispy crust, just a minute or so longer. Transfer the skillet to the oven and bake until the top is lightly browned and the frittata is firm, about 15 minutes. Carefully invert onto a festive plate. Divide, serve and share!

COMPANY COMING, OR JUST WANT TO GET THE WHOLE FAMILY INVOLVED IN cooking? These biscuits are a great weekend kitchen project and a spectacular showstopper that you can reliably pull off with a simple step-by-step plan: start the biscuits, and while they bake, make the sauce. As the biscuits finish, simply scramble the eggs, then assemble the works with the smoked salmon. Done!

SERVES 8, OR 12 WITH SMALLER PORTIONS

SMOKED SALMON BRUNCH BISCUITS

Preheat your oven to 400°F (200°C). Turn on your convection fan if you have one. Line a baking sheet with parchment paper.

In a medium bowl, whisk together the flour, baking powder, salt and pepper. Dredge the block of frozen butter in the flour, then grate it on the large holes of a box grater. (This simple method avoids the hassle of cutting the fat into the flour. More importantly, it helps to keep the fat distinct from the flour, so its water can burst into steam and work magic on the biscuits' texture.)

Gently whisk in the chives. Pour in the milk. Using the handle of a wooden spoon, vigorously stir the works together until a lump of dough forms and gathers up all the loose flour in the bowl. Fold the dough in half inside the bowl and gently flatten it. Repeat this folding and flattening step a few times to strengthen the dough. Sprinkle flour on the dough, the work surface, the rolling pin and your hands, and roll the dough out into a large, even circle about 1 inch (2.5 cm) thick, dusting with flour and flipping the dough over once or twice. Cut out 8 large or 12 smaller circles and arrange them on the baking sheet.

Bake until the biscuits are golden brown and crispy, 15 minutes or so. Rest on the baking sheet while you ready the rest of the dish.

While the biscuits bake, measure the milk, cream, cornstarch, salt and pepper into a small saucepan. Bring to a simmer, stirring, over medium-high heat until the mixture thickens into a sauce, 5 minutes or so. Crumble in the cheese and stir until the sauce is smooth. Turn off the heat and stir in the fresh dill.

Heat your favorite heavy skillet over medium-high heat. Whisk together the eggs, water, salt and pepper in a bowl. Drop the butter into the hot pan and gently swirl until golden brown and nutty-smelling. Immediately pour in the eggs. Cook, stirring with a rubber spatula or wooden spoon, until almost cooked, then remove from the heat and let the works finish cooking with their own heat.

Carefully split the freshly baked biscuits in half and arrange on plates. Divide the scrambled eggs among the biscuit bottoms. Add a layer of smoked salmon. Pour the sauce evenly over the works. Top with sprigs of fresh dill and the biscuit tops. Serve and share with a flourish!

CHIVE BISCUITS

4 cups (1 L) of all-purpose flour

2 tablespoons (30 mL) of baking powder

2 teaspoons (10 mL) of salt

Lots of freshly ground pepper

1 cup (250 mL) of butter, frozen

1 bunch of chives or green onions, thinly sliced (at least 1 cup/250 mL)

1½ cups (375 mL) of milk

BOURSIN DILL SAUCE

1 cup (250 mL) of milk

1 cup (250 mL) of whipping cream

3 tablespoons (45 mL) of cornstarch

½ teaspoon (2 mL) each of salt and pepper

1 wheel (5.2 ounces/150 g) of your favorite Boursin cheese

A handful or more of fresh dill, chopped

BROWN BUTTER SCRAMBLED EGGS

3 eggs

1 tablespoon (15 mL) of water

A pinch or two of salt

A few turns of your pepper grinder

1 tablespoon (15 mL) of butter

TO FINISH

12 slices of delicious smoked salmon, such as PEI's Medallion smoked salmon

A handful of fresh dill sprigs

LUNCHBOX
& SNACKS

FAMILY RECIPES

LUNCHBOX TIPS

10 IDEAS FOR PACKING PERFECT SCHOOL LUNCHES

1. **DON'T TEMPT FATE.** Avoid foods that have a strong smell, get soggy or fall apart easily (elaborate sandwiches, wet tomatoes or things with toppings). They're instant lunchroom turnoffs.

2. **MINI FREEZER.** A frozen juice box turns an insulated lunchbox into a little fridge. Pack one in and it'll keep the contents chilly as it slowly thaws by lunch.

3. **SMOOTHIE OF THE DAY.** Keep your blender busy with real fruit, no-sugar-added smoothies. They're perfect for a morning kick-start and a same-day lunchtime boost. I use standard-issue mason jars and post a reward for their return!

4. **BOUNTY SELLS FRUIT SALAD.** The more fruits in a fruit salad, the better it looks and tastes. Toss in all the major colors and fruits, a mixture of at least five, even ten or more, different types. For bonus points include some kind of irresistible skewer.

5. **LETTUCE WRAPS.** Wrap the works tightly in the lettuce leaves of your choice. Softer head lettuces work best. Lots of ingredients can turn into delicious lettuce wraps for lunch! Try these:

   - **TUNA WRAP.** Stir together a can of tuna, a grated carrot, a diced pickle, lemon juice, mayonnaise, hot sauce and soy sauce.

   - **CHICKEN WRAP.** Toss leftover chicken with mayonnaise, chopped apple, chopped celery, raisins and a sprinkle of curry powder.

   - **VEGGIE WRAP.** Mash an avocado with a few spoonfuls of salsa and a handful of crushed tortilla chips.

6. **IT'S ALL ABOUT THE CRUNCH.** If I'm selling something new, I always add a touch of crunch, something crispy. A handful of crisp potato chips on tuna salad or crushed tortilla chips on anything go a long way towards closing the deal, but in the big leagues we keep a bag of chow mein noodles on hand. Sprinkle them on top of anything and they'll sell!

7. **CREAM CHEESE ROLL-UPS.** Try spreading cream cheese and jelly or jam on crust-trimmed sandwich bread. Include a few berries if you like then roll the works into a tight log. Chill to firm then slice into fun rounds of flavor!

8. **APPLE SANDWICH.** You can sandwich a lot of flavor between two thick apple slices spread with peanut butter. Raisins. Dried fruit. Seeds. Nuts. Or whatever you can dream up. We really like pistachio and dried cranberry on almond butter and honeycrisp apples. Avoid nuts if it's a school requirement!

9. **HAND FRUIT.** The perfect blend of convenience, flavor and health—nothing beats a crisp apple, bright orange, ripe banana, soft peach, juicy pear or the like! Wrap a piece of paper towel around the fruit of the day, though, to ease transit. It may even end up being a napkin!

10. **CONTAINERS.** Sealable bags and spill-proof containers are an easy way to package the deal. Experience teaches us that the cook must assume responsibility for delivery of the meal and that the courier is not to be trusted.

NEED MORE LUNCHBOX RECIPE IDEAS? TRY THESE:

THIS WAS THE FIRST RECIPE I EVER INVENTED, AND WHILE I WASN'T THE FIRST TO cram a handful of crisp potato chips into a sandwich, it was the first time I discovered the thrill of edible invention. Next step? A recipe-creation career! And let's just say I've eaten a lot of these sandwiches along the way. Lately I've been dropping the sacred chips in favor of savory nori seaweed sheets—they deliver the crunch along with a special flavor boost. MAKES 2 SANDWICHES

TUNA CHIP SEAWEED SANDWICH

FOR THE TUNA SALAD

1 can (6 ounces/180 g) of water-packed
   tuna, drained

2 tablespoons (30 mL) of olive oil

1 tablespoon (15 mL) of your
   favorite mustard

1 teaspoon (5 mL) of your
   favorite vinegar

1 dill pickle, minced, or a spoonful
   of green relish

1 teaspoon (5 mL) of dried dill
   or a handful of chopped fresh

A sprinkle of salt and a few turns
   of your pepper grinder

FOR THE SANDWICHES

4 slices of artisanal bread (anything
   but bland white), toasted

A handful of crisp lettuce leaves

2 sheets of nori seaweed

A few handfuls of your favorite
   potato chips

Mix together all the ingredients for the tuna salad. Recruit your fellow sandwich eater for some of the measuring duties.

Top 2 slices of toast with a thick layer of crisp lettuce leaves. Spread the tuna salad evenly and thickly on the lettuce. Top with a savory sheet of crispy nori seaweed, and finish with a generous layer of crisp chips. Top with the last toast slices, pressing down to crush the chips into submission. Serve and share!

FAMILY FLAVORS

So much of your family's food is about the small traditions of the everyday. My kids get the same thrill I did out of the potato chips and the ritual of smashing these sandwiches into shape. Lunch and memories!

IS YOUR FAMILY IN THE SANDWICH BUSINESS? A SOFT TORTILLA WRAP IS JUST AS EASY a sandwich starter as a slice of bread. If you want to make it even easier, let your grocer do the heavy lifting and just toss a rotisserie chicken into your cart! MAKES 4 TO 6 LARGE WRAPS

ROTISSERIE CHICKEN WRAP WITH AVOCADO, TOMATOES AND BASIL

Whisk the dressing ingredients together in a medium bowl until emulsified. Use your hands or a pair of forks to pull the chicken meat from the bones and shred it into bite-size pieces. Add to the bowl along with the avocados, tomatoes and basil. Gently toss the works together.

Ready the tortillas by briefly microwaving them until soft and pliable, 30 seconds or so. Arrange the tortillas on your work surface. Place a scoop of chicken salad just below the "equator" of each. Fold the bottom of the tortilla over the filling, fold in the sides, then finish rolling. Serve and share!

FAMILY FLAVORS

Every kitchen needs time-saving strategies, and few are as effective as today's ubiquitous supermarket roast chickens. They can be a bit salty, though, so use them as a salad ingredient to help to lessen that impact.

FOR THE DRESSING

The zest and juice of 1 juicy lemon

2 tablespoons (30 mL) of olive oil

1 tablespoon (15 mL) of honey

1 tablespoon (15 mL) of your
favorite mustard

¼ teaspoon (1 mL) of salt

A few turns of your pepper grinder

FOR THE WRAP

1 rotisserie chicken, hot or chilled

2 avocados, peeled and cubed

1 pint (500 mL) of cherry tomatoes,
halved

Leaves from 1 bunch of fresh basil

4 to 6 large soft tortillas

THERE'S ALREADY A LOT OF FIBER, PROTEIN AND MICRONUTRIENTS PACKED INTO A simple can of black beans, and it's easy to add in loads of flavor and a memorable crispy crunch. All without turning on the oven! Rinsing canned beans takes away much of the added salt. MAKES 4 TO 6 WRAPS

NO-COOK SPICE-MASHED BLACK BEAN LETTUCE WRAPS

FOR THE SPICE-MASHED BEANS

A 19-ounce (540 mL) can of black beans, drained and rinsed

4 ounces (115 g) of Cheddar cheese, shredded

1 teaspoon (5 mL) of chili powder

1 teaspoon (5 mL) of ground cumin

½ teaspoon (2 mL) of your favorite hot sauce

½ teaspoon (2 mL) of salt

The zest and juice of ½ lime

FOR THE LETTUCE WRAPS

4 to 6 large leaves of Bibb or iceberg lettuce

A few spoonfuls of sour cream

A few spoonfuls of your favorite salsa

A handful of fresh cilantro sprigs

A few handfuls of corn tortilla chips

For the mashed beans, fill a medium bowl with the beans, cheese, chili powder, cumin, hot sauce, salt, and lime zest and juice. Mash and stir the works together, combining the flavors.

To craft the wraps, hold a lettuce leaf in one hand and spoon in the bright black bean filling and spoonfuls of sour cream and salsa. Top with a few sprigs of fresh cilantro, crush and crumble on the tortilla chips, wrap tightly, serve and share!

FAMILY FLAVORS

Here's a winning lunchbox strategy: pack the mashed black beans with a separate stash of lettuce leaves and toppings for on-the-go spooning 'n' rolling at the office or school. You and your kids will be the envy of the lunch crowd as you roll up the tastiest lunch in sight.

For even more variety, skip the leaves and try wrapping and rolling with tortillas or pita bread.

SOMETIMES IN LIFE, COMBINING SEVERAL NONDESCRIPT THINGS SOMEHOW CREATES something magical and memorable. The whole transcends the individual parts. This sandwich is one of those times. It's quite simply the best roast beef sandwich I've ever enjoyed! MAKES 2 SANDWICHES

ROAST BEEF AND RYE SANDWICH

Make the spread by stirring the cream cheese, horseradish and relish together in a small bowl. Evenly spread the proceeds on 2 slices of the warm toasted rye. Layer on the crisp, tangy pickles, the roast beef and the spicy arugula. Top with the remaining toast. Slice in half, serve and share!

FAMILY FLAVORS

There's no shame in hitting up one of those sandwich chains now and then. Life is busy, and sometimes our options are limited. But don't let sandwiches vanish from your homemade repertoire. A board of these beauties will remind your family that the tastiest and most soul-satisfying food is always found at home.

FOR THE SPREAD

½ cup (125 mL) of cream cheese or your favorite Boursin cheese

2 tablespoons (30 mL) of prepared horseradish

2 tablespoons (30 mL) of green relish

FOR THE SANDWICHES

4 thick slices of rye bread, toasted

2 large dill pickles, thinly sliced lengthwise

6 or 8 thin slices of the very best roast beef available

2 handfuls of arugula

EASY SNACKS

11 FUN & HEALTHY FAMILY SNACKS

1. **SNACK SHELF.** Designate a spot in your refrigerator for the snack of the day so everyone automatically knows where to look. Keep it stocked with carrot and celery sticks, broccoli and cauliflower florets and any dips you can rustle up.

2. **HUMMUS-IN-A-HURRY.** Rinse off a 540 mL/19 oz can of chickpeas, toss them in the food processor and you are moments away from a tasty batch of freestyle veggie dip. Complete the works with the juice of a lemon, enough virgin olive oil to form a smooth thick purée and whatever seasonings strike your fancy. Hummus is that easy!

3. **PITA PIZZA.** A whole-grain pita, a spoonful or two of your favorite tomato sauce, a sprinkling of grated cheese and a hot oven are all you need to make a filling snack in just minutes. For variety, try topping with different types of cheese, such as mozzarella, Cheddar, Swiss, or whatever you have on hand! Pita pizza makes a good quick lunch too!

4. **APPLE CHEDDAR QUESADILLAS.** Preheat a skillet with a bit of oil over medium heat. Lay down a whole wheat tortilla and cover the top half with grated Cheddar cheese and thinly sliced apple. Fold over and toast both sides until golden brown. This definitely can double as a great lunch idea.

5. **PEANUT BUTTER POPCORN.** Get popping! Meanwhile, melt lots of butter, then stir in an equivalent amount of peanut butter and combine before tossing the works together. For variety, try other nut butters, like almond butter or cashew butter.

6. **SMOOTHIE POPS.** Every time you bang out a batch of smoothies, make a bit more to fill up your popsicle molds. Nothing beats a healthy frozen treat on a hot summer day!

7. **YOGURT PARFAIT.** Layers of rich yogurt, today's ripe fruit and crunchy granola are irresistibly easy to turn into a snack so tasty you can call it a treat!

8. **FRUIT PIZZA.** Stir some cream cheese and jam together until well combined. Smear it on a whole-grain pita, then layer the works with sliced fruit and berries. Voila!

9. **PEANUT BUTTER & JELLY BALLS.** Stir together equal amounts of any peanut butter and your favourite jam or jelly. Add a handful of chocolate chips and enough shredded coconut and/or quick cooking oat flakes to thicken the mixture enough to form and roll into 1 inch (2 cm) balls.

10. **PEANUT BUTTER JAR.** Fill a short mason jar with a thick layer of peanut butter on the bottom then cram it full of trimmed-to-fit carrot and celery sticks for dipping.

11. **CHOCOLATE MARSHMALLOW BARK.** Try melting any amount of any chocolate, then stirring in an equivalent amount of dried fruits, nuts, candy bits or even mini marshmallows. Spread the works out in a thick layer on parchment paper, cool and crack!

NEED MORE EASY SNACK IDEAS? TRY THESE:

GABE LOVES THESE NOODLES! ALL MY KIDS LOVE SLURPY NOODLES AND SO DO I. WE especially love the convenience of packaged just-add-water instant noodles, but what's in the mysterious flavor packet? Even in a rush I just can't bring myself to use it. If you find yourself really pinched for time, buy an instant package, but lose the X-pack, keep the noodles and add your own love. MAKES ENOUGH TO FILL A 1-QUART (1 L) MASON JAR WITH A DELICIOUS MEAL-ON-THE-FLY FOR 1

JUST-ADD-WATER NOODLE JAR

2 tablespoons (30 mL) of ketchup

2 tablespoons (30 mL) of peanut butter

1 tablespoon (15 mL) of finely grated
frozen ginger

1 tablespoon (15 mL) of fish sauce

1 teaspoon (5 mL) of soy sauce

¼ teaspoon (1 mL) of your favorite
hot sauce

The zest and juice of ½ lime

1 carrot, shredded

A handful of fresh bean or lentil sprouts

A handful of shredded basil, mint and
cilantro leaves

A green onion or two, thinly sliced

1 standard-issue package (3 ounces/
85 g) of instant ramen noodles

Squeeze, spoon, splash, sprinkle and grate the ketchup, peanut butter, ginger, fish sauce, soy sauce, hot sauce, and lime zest and juice into a 1-quart (1 L) mason jar. Stir the works together. Top with the shredded carrot, bean sprouts, herbs and green onion. Before you open the noodle package, squeeze it to break up the noodles. Discard the so-called flavor packet and add the noodles to the jar.

At lunchtime, get your hands on 2 cups (500 mL) of boiling water. Pour it straight into the jar, screw the lid on tightly, fold a towel around the jar and give it a gentle shake to distribute the flavors and textures. Let rest for 10 minutes as the magic noodles soften and soak up all the surrounding flavors. Enjoy with a pair of chopsticks.

FAMILY FLAVORS

Sometimes a little bit of effort in advance brings big rewards in the future—in life and the kitchen. One of the first casualties of a busy schedule is a nutritious lunch. A quick evening rally in the kitchen will put one of these jars to bed ready to go with the promise of a delicious—and easy—lunch.

THE ONLY THING MORE DELICIOUS THAN A FRAGRANT SUN-RIPE MELON IS THE SAME melon lovingly sprinkled with a few simple seasonings. Save this one for when you're lucky enough to find a perfectly ripe, flavorful melon. Definitely one of life's great treats. SERVES 2, EVEN 3 OR 4 IN A PINCH

SALT-AND-PEPPER MELON SNACK

Cut the melon in half lengthwise and gently scoop out and discard the seeds and the stringy mass, smoothing the inside of the fruit. Cut it into quarters or eighths, then line up the pieces in a nice row on a pretty platter. Using a microplane grater, evenly dust the fruit with an aromatic shower of the citrus zest. Squeeze the juice all over the fruit too. Drizzle the works with the olive oil. Top off with flaky salt and pepper sprinkled evenly from high above. Serve with a flourish and enjoy this surprising treat!

A ripe, fragrant melon of any kind, the riper the better, and even slightly over-ripe is fine
1 lime or lemon
Generous drizzles of really good olive oil
Flakes of pretentious flaky gray sea salt
A few turns of your pepper grinder

FAMILY FLAVORS

Ripe fruit is Mother Nature's healthy treat for us—adults and kids! Fruit is the perfect after-school snack just the way it is, but why stop there? A light touch of sensible complementary flavor elevates just about any ripe fruit to true treat status.

EVERY FAMILY NEEDS A HEALTHY DIP THAT THE KIDS CAN'T KEEP THEIR CHIPS OUT of. This one could be yours. With or without the homemade pita chips, edamame beans are an inspired base for a traditionally flavored Middle Eastern hummus. SERVES A LITTLE TABLE RALLY OF 4 TO 6

EDAMAME HUMMUS WITH CURRIED PITA CHIPS

FOR THE HUMMUS

4 cups (1 L) of frozen shelled edamame

1 cup (250 mL) of water

1 teaspoon (5 mL) of salt

The zest and juice of 2 lemons

2 to 4 cloves of garlic

½ cup (125 mL) of tahini

¼ cup (60 mL) of your very best
   olive oil

1 teaspoon (5 mL) of your favorite
   hot sauce

FOR THE PITA CHIPS

1 tablespoon (15 mL) of curry powder

2 tablespoons (30 mL) of good olive oil

2 tablespoons (30 mL) of honey

4 or 5 pita breads

Fine sea salt and a few turns of your
   pepper grinder

Preheat your oven to 350°F (180°C). Turn on your convection fan if you have one and some music if you like.

For the hummus, pour the edamame, water and salt into a saucepan. Bring to a slow, steady simmer over medium-high heat; simmer until the edamame soften, 10 minutes max. Pour the works into the bowl of your food processor. Add the lemon zest and juice, garlic, tahini, oil and hot sauce. Pulse until smoothly and evenly textured and brightly colored. Set aside while you turn your attention to the pita chips.

Measure the curry powder, then the oil and finally the honey into a coffee cup. (The honey won't stick to the oiled measuring spoon.) Microwave just long enough to melt the honey a bit, 15 seconds or so. Stir together with a pastry brush. Brush thoroughly and evenly over the top of each pita. Sprinkle lightly with salt and pepper. Stack the pitas, then cut the pile into 6 wedges. Spread the wedges in a single layer on a baking sheet. Bake until each and every one is golden brown, 15 minutes or so, maybe 20 in a slower oven. Cool completely. Spoon the hummus into your nicest bowl, arrange the chips around it, and serve and share!

FAMILY FLAVORS

A dish like this can be part of your standard family repertoire in both flavor and spirit, not only your go-to for entertaining but the "company's coming" signal to the kids to keep their hands to themselves and be good hosts, even actively engaged waiters passing hors d'oeuvres. After all, there's a little bit of love in sharing something special.

MUFFINS ARE ONE OF THE EASIEST WAYS TO GET YOUR TOES WET IN THE SHALLOW end of the baking pool before diving into the big league of pies and pastries. Stirring the spirit of a great granola into the works adds an extra dimension of morning power. MAKES 12 MUFFINS

GRANOLA MUFFINS

Preheat your oven to 400°F (200°C). Turn on your convection fan if you have one. Line a muffin pan with paper liners.

In a large bowl, whisk together the flour, cinnamon, baking powder and salt. Add half of the granola, gently stirring to preserve its texture. In a medium bowl, whisk together the eggs, sugar, milk, vegetable oil, vanilla, and orange zest and juice. Pour the wet into the dry and stir the works together just until an even batter forms.

Evenly distribute the batter among the muffin cups. (Use two soupspoons to speed the process, one to scoop, one to scrape.) Evenly sprinkle the muffins with the remaining granola. Bake until risen and deliciously golden brown, 15 minutes or so. A toothpick inserted into the center should emerge clean and crumb-free. Turn muffins out of the pan and cool on racks.

2 cups (500 mL) of all-purpose flour
1 tablespoon (15 mL) of cinnamon
1 tablespoon (15 mL) of baking powder
1 teaspoon (5 mL) of salt
2 cups (500 mL) of your
  favorite granola
2 eggs
1 cup (250 mL) of white sugar
1 cup (250 mL) of milk
½ cup (125 mL) of vegetable oil
1 tablespoon (15 mL) of pure
  vanilla extract
The zest and juice of 1 orange

FAMILY FLAVORS

Muffins are a treat for everyone, especially when they're simultaneously hearty, healthy, delicious and engaging. They're reliably easy to make, so encourage your resident bakers to try their hand at creating their own version. Let them know that any breakfast cereal can replace the granola.

GENIUS! A DELICIOUSLY ADDICTIVE SNACK THAT'S ALSO GOOD FOR YOU. KALE CHIPS are awesome, and it's no wonder they're suddenly mainstream. And they're so easy to make and enjoy at home. SERVES 4 AS A SNACK, BUT YOU REALLY SHOULD JUST GO AHEAD AND DOUBLE THE WORKS—YOU'LL BE GLAD YOU DID

SPICY KALE CHIPS

1 tablespoon (15 mL) of any oil

2 teaspoons (10 mL) of soy sauce

½ teaspoon (2 mL) of your favorite hot sauce

A very large bunch of dark green kale

FAMILY FLAVORS

You really have to work hard at home to counter the relentless competition of the snack food industry and convince your kids that there exist tasty snacks beyond fries and chips. Not every kid will go for it, but some will. It's worth trying! Worst-case scenario? Memories of the best healthy snack you ever tried!

Preheat your oven to 300°F (150°C). Turn on your convection fan if you have one. Line a baking sheet with parchment paper or a nonstick baking mat.

Whisk together the oil, soy sauce and hot sauce in a large bowl. Trim each kale leaf from its tough center stem and cut into 4 roughly even pieces. Toss the pieces with the seasoned oil, coating them thoroughly, then spread the works in an even layer on the baking sheet.

Bake for 15 minutes or so, then flip the leaves over. Continue baking for 10 minutes or so, until the kale is very dry, light and crisp. Serve and share!

THIS INCREDIBLE TREAT IS THE PERFECT SNACK—SALTY, CRUNCHY, TASTY AND SO addictive. There's never enough of these darn things. They always run out! MAKES MORE THAN A POUND (450 G) OF CRUNCHY GOODNESS

SPICY SALTY SEEDY NUTS

Line a baking sheet with parchment paper and lightly oil the paper. In a large bowl, toss together your choice of nuts and seeds with the baking soda, coating the works evenly.

Pour the water into a large saucepan. Add the sugar in a small, tight pile in the center of the water. Don't stir! Heat over medium-high heat. The sugar will quickly dissolve into the water and form a simple syrup. Stirring causes small bits of sugar to splash on the side of the pot, where they can crystallize and turn the whole syrup gritty.

As the temperature increases, the syrup will begin simmering and steaming, and the water will gradually evaporate. Once the water's gone, the temperature will continue to rise and the sugar will start to turn golden.

When you see the first hint of golden brown, begin gently swirling the pan, helping the caramel color evenly. When the caramel is deep golden brown—as brown as you dare—add the butter and carefully whisk it in until the sauce is smooth. Immediately dump in the nuts and seeds, vigorously stirring the works together. The heat will activate the baking soda, releasing an eruption of tiny CO_2 bubbles that will permeate the works with a network of weak points as it cools and hardens. Brittle. Brilliant.

Use a wooden spoon to guide the hot, foamy mixture onto the baking sheet, spreading and smoothing it into a thin layer. As soon as possible, sprinkle evenly with salt and pepper. Cool completely. Crack and crumble into easily shared snack shards. In the unlikely event of leftovers, store in an airtight bag or container.

3 cups (750 mL) of your favorite nuts and seeds
1 teaspoon (5 mL) of baking soda
1 cup (250 mL) of water
2 cups (500 mL) of white sugar
1 tablespoon (15 mL) of butter
1 teaspoon (5 mL) of fine or flaky sea salt
A few turns of your pepper grinder

FAMILY FLAVORS

You don't stand a chance with this snack. Once you discover how easy it is to make, and once your kids get wind of how tasty it is, you'll be on the hook for regular batches. No worries. Add experimentation to the mix by getting your kids to customize the nut and seed blend.

SIMPLE
SALADS

FAMILY RECIPES

THIS IS A SALAD FOR PEOPLE WHO THINK THEY DON'T LIKE SALAD. IF IT TAKES A FEW bacon slices to counteract vegetable phobia, then so be it. Does the end justify the means in the kitchen? You can discuss amongst yourselves as the salad disappears! SERVES 4 TO 6

BACON SALAD WITH CRISPY ONIONS

FOR THE DRESSING

8 thick slices of bacon

3 tablespoons (45 mL) of cider vinegar

1 tablespoon (15 mL) of Dijon mustard

1 tablespoon (15 mL) of honey

¼ teaspoon (1 mL) of salt

Lots of freshly ground pepper

FOR THE SALAD

½ head of iceberg lettuce, thinly sliced
　or chopped

1 or 2 carrots, shredded

A few radishes, shredded

2 green onions, thinly sliced

A handful of chopped fresh parsley

1 pint (500 mL) of cherry
　tomatoes, halved

1 cup (250 mL) of canned crispy
　fried onions

Begin the dressing by slowly and patiently browning and crisping the bacon in a large skillet over medium heat. Take your time, and you'll be rewarded with magnificent bacon crisps and lots of rendered fat. Drain the bacon on paper towels, reserving the fat.

In a festive salad bowl, whisk together up to ⅓ cup (75 mL) of the bacon fat (save the rest to flavor something else), vinegar, mustard, honey, salt and pepper. Add the lettuce, carrots, radishes, green onions, parsley, and tomatoes. (You may make the salad to this point an hour or two ahead. Cover and chill.)

Just before serving, toss everything together, evenly mixing the flavors, textures and colors. Top with crispy onions and artfully arranged bacon slices. Serve and share!

FAMILY FLAVORS
- - - - - - - - - - - -
Fussy eaters? Here's your salad strategy: First break out the big guns—the bacon, the secret ingredient that can be counted on to get your kids eating salad. Get 'em hooked, then gradually morph the bacon fat in the dressing into much healthier olive oil. Will they notice? I'm not telling!

THE DISTINCTIVE BRIGHT INGREDIENTS OF THE SUNNY SOUTHWEST STAR IN THIS celebration of salad flavors, colors and textures. There's a lot to love here, and it's so easy to toss together in a hurry! SERVES 2 AS A FULL MEAL, 4 AS A SIDE DISH OR 6 AS A SIDE SALAD

SUNNY SOUTHWESTERN SALAD

Make the tortilla crisps first. Preheat your oven to 350°F (180°C). Turn on your convection fan if you have one. Cut each tortilla in half, stack the halves, and slice into long, thin strips, as evenly and thinly as possible. Spread the strips on a baking sheet and bake until every last one is golden brown and crisp, 10 to 15 minutes. Cool on the baking sheet.

While the crisps cool, make the dressing. In a festive salad bowl, whisk together the sour lime, smooth oil, sweet honey, aromatic cumin, spicy hot sauce and salt. Add the snappy arugula, the green onions, cilantro, avocados, bell pepper, corn and cheese. Toss the works together, evenly mixing the flavors, textures and colors. Top with the crisp tortillas. Serve and share with a bright sunny smile!

FOR CRUNCHY TEXTURE

2 large flour or corn tortillas

FOR THE DRESSING

The zest and juice of 2 limes

1 tablespoon (15 mL) of olive oil

1 tablespoon (15 mL) of honey

1 teaspoon (5 mL) of ground cumin

1 teaspoon (5 mL) of your favorite
   hot sauce

½ teaspoon (2 mL) of salt

FOR THE SALAD

A big handful of arugula for everyone

2 bunches of green onions, thinly sliced

2 handfuls of fresh cilantro leaves
   and tender stems

2 avocados, peeled and chopped

1 red bell pepper, diced

1 cup (250 mL) of corn kernels, raw or
   cooked, fresh or frozen, hot or cold

1 cup (250 mL) of shredded
   Cheddar cheese

FAMILY FLAVORS

It can be fun to plate your dinner restaurant-style now and then. Show your kids how just a flourish or two can elevate food into the realm of edible art. This salad can be tossed and served family-style in a large bowl, but it can also be dressed up considerably by keeping the various elements separate and artfully arranging them on individual plates. Same taste but a whole different vibe—especially if it helps you recruit a sous-chef or two!

YOU DON'T NEED GREENS TO MAKE AN AWESOME SALAD. THIS CRISP SALAD REVEALS the versatility of a great apple as an anchor for lots of balanced flavors. Carrot ribbons add colorful texture and flavor, distinctive pumpkin seeds bring a rustic crunchy note, and fresh bursts of mint and chewy raisins round out the works—but apple remains the core! SERVES 4 TO 6

APPLE CARROT PUMPKIN SEED SALAD WITH CIDER DRESSING

FOR THE SALAD

2 cups (500 mL) of pumpkin seeds

4 crisp apples (unpeeled), the more
   local and fresh the better

½ red onion, very thinly sliced

2 carrots, peeled into thin ribbons with
   a vegetable peeler

1 cup (125 mL) of raisins

A few handfuls of fresh mint leaves

FOR THE DRESSING

2 tablespoons (30 mL) of cider vinegar

2 tablespoons (30 mL) of olive oil

2 tablespoons (30 mL) of honey

1 tablespoon (15 mL) of your
   favorite mustard

1 teaspoon (5 mL) of ground allspice
   or cinnamon

½ teaspoon (2 mL) of salt

Preheat your oven to 350°F (180°C). Bake the pumpkin seeds on a baking sheet to remove any shelf staleness, crisping and toasting them a bit along the way, about 15 minutes.

In a festive salad bowl, smoothly whisk together the dressing ingredients until emulsified.

Stand each apple upright and cut from top to bottom beside the core. Cut off the opposite side, then cut off the two middle pieces. Slice the apple pieces as thinly as possible. Add to the dressing along with the red onion, carrots, raisins, mint leaves and the pumpkin seeds. Toss the works together, evenly mixing the flavors, textures and colors. Serve and share!

FAMILY FLAVORS

This is a perfect lunchbox salad because, unlike a bowl of dressed greens, this one doesn't wilt. It actually gets better overnight, so the next day it will be the envy of the lunchroom.

Y KIDS LOVE PICKLES SO MUCH THAT I CREATED THIS SALAD AS A HOMAGE TO THEIR favorite crunchy sour treat. It's a fun way to honor the sacred pickle's rightful place in our hearts and on our table. It's delicious too! MAKES 2 BIG OR 4 SMALLER SIDE SALADS

PICKLE SALAD WITH PICKLE DRESSING

To make the dressing, splash 1 tablespoon (15 mL) of the oil into a small skillet. Spoon in the coriander seeds and fennel seeds. Toast them, stirring, over medium-high heat until they begin to sizzle, loudly announcing that vigorous heat has chased away any shelf staleness. Cool! Cool.

In a medium bowl, combine the colorful relish, sour vinegar, remaining 1 tablespoon (15 mL) of smooth oil, sweet honey, sharp yet magically emulsifying mustard, spicy hot sauce and salt. Whisk until emulsified. Stir in the fragrant spice seeds.

Add the cucumber, dill pickles, red onion and dill. Toss the works together, evenly mixing the flavors, textures and colors. Serve and share!

FAMILY FLAVORS

Your kitchen is full of magic and mystery that just might razzle and dazzle any budding scientist hanging around. Let them whisk the dressing without the mustard and watch it slowly separate. Then whisk it with the mustard and see what happens. Send your young scientist off to explore "emulsifier," and enjoy the answer along with the salad!

FOR THE DRESSING

2 tablespoons (30 mL) of olive oil
1 tablespoon (15 mL) of coriander seeds
1 tablespoon (15 mL) of fennel seeds
2 tablespoons (30 mL) of green relish
1 tablespoon (15 mL) of cider vinegar
1 tablespoon (15 mL) of honey
1 tablespoon (15 mL) of yellow mustard
½ teaspoon (2 mL) of your favorite
  hot sauce
¼ teaspoon (1 mL) of sea salt

FOR THE SALAD

1 English cucumber (unpeeled), diced
2 large dill pickles, diced
½ red onion, thinly sliced
A handful of fresh dill, chopped

A GOOD OLD-FASHIONED POTATO SALAD IS NOT THE SORT OF THING THAT NEEDS reinventing or tampering with. You also can't screw it up, because it's really just a way to dress up leftover cooked potatoes. All the basics are here, with a tangy twist or two. SERVES 4 TO 6

POTATO SALAD WITH HORSERADISH DRESSING

FOR THE SALAD

2 pounds (900 g) of your favorite
  raw or leftover cooked potatoes
  (unpeeled)
4 dill pickles, diced
2 celery ribs, diced
4 green onions, thinly sliced
A handful of chopped fresh parsley

FOR THE DRESSING

2 tablespoons (30 mL) of mayonnaise
2 tablespoons (30 mL) of prepared
  horseradish
2 tablespoons (30 mL) of white vinegar
½ teaspoon (2 mL) of salt
¼ teaspoon (1 mL) of your favorite
  hot sauce

Steam, boil or bake the raw potatoes until they're tender, 20 to 40 minutes depending on their size. When they're cool enough to handle, cut into small bite-size pieces.

While the potatoes cook, in a large bowl, whisk together the dressing ingredients. Add the potato pieces, pickles, celery, green onions and parsley. Toss the works together, evenly mixing the flavors, textures and colors. Feel free to make the salad a day or two in advance. Serve and share!

FAMILY FLAVORS

Your kids are going to spend the rest of their lives remembering your potato salad and comparing it to every other potato salad they eat. Better make yours a good one! This recipe is hard to top. The earthy potatoes are balanced with a smooth, tangy dressing and lots of bright green flavor.

CALLING THIS SALAD A SLAW IS LIKE CALLING A ROLLS-ROYCE A CAR. THE BEAUTY is in the details: the ethereal vanilla in the dressing, the finesse of the bitter leaves, the exotic made approachable. Drive on! SERVES 6 TO 8, WITH LEFTOVERS

FANCY SLAW

In a large bowl, whisk together the dressing ingredients. Throw in the endives, radicchio, apple, pine nuts, raisins and tarragon. Toss the works together, evenly mixing the flavors, textures and colors. Serve and share!

FAMILY FLAVORS

Anyone can bring home plain old romaine from the supermarket, but it takes confidence to haul Belgian endive and radicchio. Strut your stuff and show off the goods. Maybe a couple extra laps up and down the candy aisle. You know the one, don't you?

FOR THE DRESSING

¼ cup (60 mL) of olive oil

¼ cup (60 mL) of honey

½ cup (125 mL) of white wine vinegar

½ teaspoon (2 mL) of pure
  vanilla extract

1 teaspoon (5 mL) of sea salt

½ teaspoon (2 mL) of your favorite
  hot sauce

FOR THE SALAD

2 Belgian endives, leaves trimmed,
  stacked and thinly sliced

1 radicchio, leaves trimmed, stacked
  and thinly sliced

1 crisp apple (unpeeled), cut into
  matchstick pieces

½ cup (125 mL) of pine nuts or
  slivered almonds

½ cup (125 mL) of raisins

Leaves from 1 bunch of fresh tarragon

THERE ARE A LOT OF REASONS WHY PIZZA IS SO ADDICTIVE, AND A LOT OF THOSE reasons are in this salad. No matter how these familiar flavors arrive, they always show up delicious!

SERVES 2 AS A MAIN OR 4 AS A SIDE SALAD

PIZZA SALAD

FOR THE CRISPY, CHEWY CROUTONS

4 slices of prosciutto

4 thick slices of artisanal bread,
  cut into small bite-size cubes

2 tablespoons (30 mL) of water

1 tablespoon (15 mL) of olive oil

FOR THE DRESSING

2 tablespoons (30 mL) of olive oil

1 tablespoon (15 mL) of
  balsamic vinegar

1 tablespoon (15 mL) of Dijon mustard

1 teaspoon (5 mL) of dried oregano

FOR THE SALAD

1 pint (500 mL) of cherry tomatoes,
  halved

8 ounces (225 g) of mini bocconcini
  cheese, drained

Leaves from 1 bunch of fresh basil

Preheat your oven to 350°F (180°C). Turn on your convection fan if you have one. Line a baking sheet with parchment paper and lightly oil the paper.

Arrange the prosciutto slices at one end of the baking sheet. In a large bowl, quickly toss the bread with the water until the moisture is evenly absorbed. Splash in the oil and toss again until evenly coated. (The water on the inside helps the croutons stay chewy, while the oil on the outside adds crispiness.) Spread out on the other end of the baking sheet. Bake, stirring once halfway through, until the croutons are golden brown and crispy, about 15 minutes.

Meanwhile, wipe out the bowl and in it whisk together the dressing ingredients until emulsified. Throw in the cherry tomatoes, bocconcini and basil leaves. Sprinkle on the croutons and crumble in the prosciutto. Toss the works together, evenly mixing the flavors, textures and colors. Serve, share and enjoy a little piece of Italy in your very own kitchen!

FAMILY FLAVORS

Sometimes success at the dinner table is all about clever marketing. Never underestimate the power of a good name to help achieve licked-clean plates. Which would you prefer to eat? "White Cheese Tomato Salad with Bread and Green Basil"? Or "Pizza Salad"?

MAKING TABBOULEH TRANSFORMS COOKED WHOLE GRAINS INTO A DELICIOUS AND nutritious salad. Toss in lots of green flavor and a bright lemony dressing and you're well on your way to a classic Mediterranean side dish. Add a barley-kale twist or two along the way and stand by for empty bowls! SERVES 4 TO 6, WITH LEFTOVERS

BARLEY KALE TABBOULEH

Stack the kale leaves, then roll them up tightly. Slice them as thinly as possible, forming fine threads. Cram into a small saucepan and add ¼ cup (60 mL) of water. Cover and cook over high heat until the kale softens, just 2 or 3 minutes. Drain and spread out on a plate to cool.

Measure the barley into the same saucepan and add 3 cups (750 mL) of water and the salt. Bring to a full boil, then reduce the heat to a bare simmer. Cover tightly and continue cooking until the grains swell, absorbing the water and tenderizing, about 30 minutes.

Meanwhile, in a large bowl, whisk together the dressing ingredients until emulsified. Throw in the tender barley, the kale, parsley, mint, green onions, tomatoes and pickle. Toss the works together, evenly mixing the flavors, textures and colors. Serve and share!

FAMILY FLAVORS
- - - - - - - - - - -
Part of being the family cook is recognizing your whole-grain responsibilities. It's your job to regularly find ways to include these nutrition powerhouses among the everyday flavors of life. A simple salad is one way to slip them past the ever-so-vigilant gatekeepers at your table.

FOR THE SALAD

4 large kale leaves, tough center
   stems trimmed away
1 cup (250 mL) of any barley
1 teaspoon (5 mL) of salt
A handful of finely chopped
   fresh parsley
Leaves from 1 bunch of fresh mint,
   finely chopped
4 green onions, thinly sliced
1 pint (500 mL) of cherry
   tomatoes, halved
1 large dill pickle, minced

FOR THE DRESSING

The zest and juice of 1 lemon
2 tablespoons (30 mL) of olive oil
1 tablespoon (15 mL) of honey
1 tablespoon (15 mL) of your
   favorite mustard
½ teaspoon (2 mL) of salt
½ teaspoon (2 mL) of your favorite
   hot sauce

THE FLAVORS OF A CLASSIC GREEK SALAD WOULD BE CLASSIC NO MATTER WHERE they came from because they're just plain delicious no matter how you mix them. Or what you mix into them. A delicious twist of tender, nutritionally dense quinoa? Sure!

QUINOA GREEK SALAD

FOR THE QUINOA

1 cup (250 mL) of any quinoa
2 cups (500 mL) of water
½ teaspoon (2 mL) of salt

FOR THE DRESSING

The zest and juice of 2 lemons
2 tablespoons (30 mL) of olive oil
1 tablespoon (15 mL) of yellow mustard
1 tablespoon (15 mL) of honey
½ teaspoon (2 mL) of salt
½ teaspoon (2 mL) of your favorite
   hot sauce

FOR THE SALAD

1 large English cucumber
   (unpeeled), diced
1 red bell pepper, diced
1 red onion, diced
8 to 12 ounces (225 to 340 g)
   of feta cheese, drained and
   cubed or crumbled
1 cup (250 mL) of pistachios
Leaves from a large bunch of fresh mint

Rinse the quinoa under cold running water, then drain. Pour into a small saucepan along with the water and salt. Bring to a steady simmer, then reduce the heat to a bare simmer, cover tightly and simmer until tender, about 20 minutes. Turn off the heat and let rest for 5 minutes before removing the lid.

Meanwhile, in a large bowl, whisk together the dressing ingredients until emulsified. Add the cucumber, red pepper, red onion, feta and pistachios. Tear in the mint. Spoon in the steaming quinoa. Toss the works together, evenly mixing the flavors, textures and colors. Serve and share!

FAMILY FLAVORS

One of the best strategies for efficient home cooking is a big weekend rally. Spend a few hours of a Sunday afternoon making a batch or two of tricks-up-your-sleeve dishes that will deliver a week of family lunches ahead. Dishes like this salad. Rock like a deli cook making the special-of-the-day. Here's the plan: Get the quinoa cooking. While it cooks, whisk the dressing and craft the rest of the salad. Done!

THE BIGGEST INFLUENCE SOUTHEAST ASIAN COOKS HAVE ON OTHER COOKS IS THEIR instinctive balanced approach to layering flavor: sweet, sour, salty, savory and spicy. Together, the brightest flavors on the planet. SERVES 4 TO 6 HAPPY TABLEMATES

SHANGHAI BEAN SALAD WITH TORN NORI

To start the salad, trim the stem end from the beans, leaving the cute little curlicue at the other end intact. Halve the beans and fit into a small saucepan with a few splashes of water. Cover and steam over medium-high until bright green and tender-crisp, 1 or 2 minutes. Drain, rinse with cold water to stop the cooking, and drain again.

In a large bowl, whisk together the dressing ingredients until smooth. Add the green beans, bean sprouts, red pepper, green onions and cashews. Toss the works together, evenly mixing the flavors, textures and colors. Top with the crunchy onions and torn nori. Serve and share with chopsticks!

FAMILY FLAVORS

Every family should know how to use chopsticks, and it's up to the parents to lead the charge. Any time you get near the flavors of Southeast Asia, just whip out the sticks and get to fiddling. In no time flat you'll be ready for dim-sum brunch at your local Chinese restaurant. Of course, cutlery is always an option!

FOR THE SALAD

12 ounces (340 g) of green beans

12 ounces (340 g) of bean sprouts

1 red bell pepper, sliced as thinly as possible

4 green onions, thinly sliced

1 cup (250 mL) of cashews

1 cup (250 mL) of canned crispy fried onions

4 sheets of nori seaweed, torn

FOR THE DRESSING

1 inch (2.5 cm) of frozen ginger, finely grated

1 tablespoon (15 mL) of ketchup

1 tablespoon (15 mL) of white, cider or rice vinegar

1 tablespoon (15 mL) of soy sauce

1 tablespoon (15 mL) of fish sauce

1 tablespoon (15 mL) of honey

1 teaspoon (5 mL) of toasted sesame oil

½ teaspoon (2 mL) of your favorite hot sauce

COOK
AHEAD

EVERY HOUSE NEEDS A RED SAUCE—YOUR BASIC TASTY TOMATO PURÉE FOR EVERY day. The standby sauce that can turn any pasta and garnish into a meal in minutes. A sauce you can bang out in the time it takes the water to boil and the noodles to cook. So start the clock and start cooking!

SERVES 4 TO 6, WITH LEFTOVERS

HOUSE RED SAUCE

2 or 3 tablespoons (30 or 45 mL)
    of olive oil

4 large onions, finely chopped

Cloves from 1 head of garlic, sliced

2 cans (28 ounces/796 mL each)
    of crushed tomatoes

A 14-ounce (398 mL) can of
    tomato paste

2 cups (500 mL) of big red wine

1 tablespoon (15 mL) of red
    wine vinegar

1 tablespoon (15 mL) of dried oregano

2 bay leaves

½ teaspoon (2 mL) of salt

Lots of freshly ground pepper

Splash the oil into a large saucepan over medium-high heat. Toss in the onions and garlic as you finish prepping them. Stir-fry until the proceeds are golden brown, sizzling and smell delicious, 10 minutes or so.

Add the crushed tomatoes, tomato paste, wine, vinegar, oregano, bay leaves, salt and pepper. Stir the works as it comes to a slow, steady simmer.

As soon as the sauce is simmering hot, it's ready to enjoy, perhaps with some simultaneously cooked pasta and some vegetables. Feel free to simmer a bit longer, though, further developing and deepening the flavors. Reserve half the tasty proceeds for another meal. Serve and share, imagining the possibilities awaiting in your refrigerator or freezer!

Store in a tightly sealed jar or container for 7 days in your refrigerator or 1 month in your freezer.

FAMILY FLAVORS

It's just as easy to make a lot as a little. Double this recipe and you'll magically have a batch of tasty homemade sauce ready for another meal or two. That credo applies to much of cooking, and over time you'll improve your family's kitchen efficiency. It's a good feeling to have a freezer full of meal options for a future busy day.

IT DOESN'T TAKE MUCH COAXING FOR HAM HOCKS TO FLAVOR THE SORT OF RICH, tasty broth that guarantees soup success. A steady hot bath is all they'll need, with earthy lentils along for the ride. Finish with an aromatic flourish to fill your bowl with flavor. MAKES ENOUGH FOR A GOOD FEED FOR 4 TO 6

HAM HOCK LENTIL SOUP

Toss the ham hock, bay leaves and salt into a large pot and submerge in the water. Bring to a slow, steady simmer, then cover and continue cooking until the meat is tender and the broth is rich, at least an hour, maybe two.

Stir in the carrot, onion, celery, garlic and lentils. Cover and continue cooking until the delicious legumes are tender, another hour or so.

Lift the hock onto a plate or cutting board. Discard the skin and fat, and tug and pull the meat from the bone into small bite-size pieces. Return the meat to the pot and reheat.

Just before serving, stir in the fresh aromatic herb and the sharp mustard and vinegar, brightening and balancing the flavors. Ladle, serve and share!

A big fat smoked ham hock

2 bay leaves

2 teaspoons (10 mL) of salt

12 cups (2.8 L) of water

1 large carrot, chopped

1 large onion, chopped

2 celery ribs, chopped

Cloves from 1 head of garlic, thinly sliced

2 cups (500 mL) of green lentils

1 heaping tablespoon (20 mL) or more of minced fresh thyme, tarragon, sage, rosemary or oregano

1 tablespoon (15 mL) of Dijon mustard

1 teaspoon (5 mL) of cider vinegar

FAMILY FLAVORS

Sometimes life sneaks in sniffles and sneezes. When you need a warm bowl of comforting soup, this is the one for you. Hearty, nourishing and filling, with the sort of flavor you tend to crave whenever you need a boost. The kitchen doctor is in the house and on duty!

THE DEEPEST, BEEFIEST GOODNESS ISN'T STEAK. IT'S FOUND IN A FEW CHOICE tougher cuts through patient browning and braising. Harness the power of patience and fill your pot with simmering goodness. You'll be rewarded with soul-satisfying flavor. Enjoy as is or freestyle a flavor theme. Either way, you'll love the true beefy flavor of this broth. FUELS 4, MAYBE 6 IF YOU STRETCH IT

BEEFY BROTH

A big splash of vegetable oil,
  preferably grapeseed
2 pounds (900 g) or more of beef short
  ribs, oxtails or beef shanks
2 carrots, coarsely chopped
2 celery ribs, coarsely chopped
2 onions, sliced
A 28-ounce (796 mL) can of any type
  of tomatoes (whole, crushed, diced
  or puréed)
4 cups (1 L) of water or, if you're
  feeling extravagant, 1 bottle of big,
  beefy good red wine
A bay leaf or two
A handful of fresh thyme or
  rosemary sprigs
1 teaspoon (5 mL) of salt
A few turns of your pepper grinder

Preheat your oven to 250°F (120°C).

Pour a pool of oil into your favorite heavy ovenproof pot over medium-high heat. Dry the beef on paper towels, then use tongs to carefully place pieces in the sizzling oil. Don't crowd the pan, or the meat won't brown. Listen to the heat. A simmering pan means nothing. Sizzle is the sound of flavor. Too loud, though, and a sizzling pan becomes a smoking-burning pan. When the beef is deeply browned all over, transfer it to a plate. Repeat with the rest of the beef, 10 to 15 minutes in total. Pour off any excess oil, leaving behind any browned bits of goodness. Toss all the beef and any accumulated juices back in the pot.

To this beefy goodness, add the carrots, celery, onions, tomatoes, water, bay leaves, herb sprigs, salt and pepper. Bring to a slow, steady simmer, then cover tightly. Transfer to the oven and braise for 3 to 4 hours, stirring now and then, tenderizing the meat, releasing the richness and building deep beefy flavor. Pour in some extra water if need be. (Alternatively, you can simmer the pot on your stovetop. You may find that even your lowest heat is still too much, though, so try offsetting your pot a bit from the heat so the liquid doesn't evaporate too quickly.) Slip out the bones toward the end.

Serve and share exactly as is, or season and garnish any way you care to. Add any flavor theme and its accompanying vegetables, as elaborate as you care to be or as simple as you need to be. Use the broth in a soup, stew or sauce. Store the broth in a tightly sealed jar or container for 7 days in your refrigerator or 1 month in your freezer.

FAMILY FLAVORS

There are as many ways to fill your bowl with beefy stew as there are cooks and flavors. The possibilities are endless. I like to stir in a can of drained, rinsed chickpeas, some just-cooked pasta and a tote of baby spinach. Making this broth offers a lesson in patience for any sous-chefs in your brigade. Patience for life and the kitchen. With time comes tenderness.

YOU CAN MAKE A BATCH OF THIS BEEFY GOODNESS IN A HURRY IF YOU HAVE TO, OR plan ahead and stock a big batch in the freezer. Either way, you're no more than a few minutes away from a quick round of drop-in sandwiches for a gang of teenagers or even old-timer wannabe teenagers.

MAKES A 2-POUND (900 G) BATCH, ENOUGH FOR 12 TO 16 SANDWICHES

BIG BATCH OF SLOPPY JOES

Place your favorite heavy pot over medium-high heat. Pour in the oil and toss in the onions, red peppers, celery and garlic. Sizzle and stir them as they soften and their flavors brighten, a few minutes. Stir in the chili powder, cumin and salt. Cook for another minute to brighten their flavors.

Stir in the meat, vigorously breaking it up into much smaller pieces. Don't brown the meat—that toughens it. When the meat is no longer pink, add the tomatoes, tomato paste, vinegar and hot sauce. Bring to a slow, steady simmer, stirring as you go.

Freeze for future goodness, or spoon onto fresh soft bun bottoms, cover with their bun tops, serve and share!

2 tablespoons (30 mL) of vegetable oil

2 large onions, finely chopped

2 red bell peppers, diced

4 celery ribs, finely chopped

Cloves from 1 head of garlic, finely chopped

2 tablespoons (30 mL) of chili powder

2 tablespoons (30 mL) of ground cumin

2 teaspoons (10 mL) of salt

2 pounds (900 g) of fatty ground beef

2 cans (28 ounces/796 mL each) of diced tomatoes

2 cans (5.5 ounces/156 mL) of tomato paste

1 tablespoon (15 mL) of red wine vinegar

2 teaspoons (10 mL) of your favorite hot sauce

FAMILY FLAVORS

There's no real finesse to a mess of sloppy joes. This purely functional method is fast and furious and packs a satisfying punch of flavor. Just what you need in a real-world kitchen.

COOK ONCE, EAT TWICE. ONE STEW SETS YOU UP FOR TWO DIFFERENT MEALS: A classic country pork stew and a downtown version with big-city flavors of the world. At heart this is a simple pork shoulder braised with classic garden vegetables. Half the fun the first time is imagining how you'll transform the leftovers with stir-in flavors and finishing flourishes. MAKES ENOUGH TENDER, FLAVORFUL STEW FOR 4 TO 6 TO FEAST TWICE

COUNTRY STEW, CITY STEW

2 tablespoons (30 mL) of vegetable oil

A large pork shoulder (4 pounds/1.8 kg or so), cut in half

2 celery ribs, diced

2 carrots, diced

2 onions, diced

2 big potatoes, any kind, peeled if you prefer, diced

2 bay leaves

A spoonful of dried thyme or rosemary

1 teaspoon (5 mL) of salt

8 cups (2 L) of water

FAMILY FLAVORS

Efficiency is the name of the game when you're running a busy family kitchen. One stew rally yields tonight's dinner as well as a leg up on another dinner soon. That's a winning strategy!

Preheat your oven to 300°F (150°C). Turn on your convection fan if you have one.

Pour a pool of oil into your favorite heavy ovenproof pot over medium-high heat. Dry the pork shoulder with paper towels, then use tongs to carefully place it in the sizzling oil and begin browning it. Don't crowd the pan, or the meat won't brown. Listen to the heat. A simmering pan means nothing. Sizzle is the sound of flavor. Too loud, though, and a sizzling pan becomes a smoking-burning pan. Cook until the pork is nicely browned all over, 10 to 15 minutes.

Add the celery, carrots, onions, potatoes, bay leaves, thyme, salt and water. Bring to a steady simmer, then cover tightly and transfer to the oven. Braise for 3 hours or so, until the meat melts into submission and a rich, hearty broth forms. Don't worry about overcooking—the meat just gets more and more tender with time.

Serve and share half as is, straightaway, sliced, shredded or cut it into chunks. Refrigerate or freeze the leftovers.

Next meal, dump the leftovers into a stew pot with a splash or two of water and stir over medium-high heat until simmering and delicious again. Enjoy as is once again, or enjoy getting creative. Stir in your choice of flavors and aromatic flourishes: condiments, spices, herbs, vegetables, tomatoes, hearty fruits, canned beans, pastas, savory greens and anything else you can think of.

To store, refrigerate in a tightly sealed jar or container for 7 days or 1 month in your freezer.

ROAST A CHICKEN OVER A BED OF VEGETABLES, QUICKLY SHRED THE MEAT AND enjoy your first meal. Then make a broth with the carcass and turn the leftovers into soup tomorrow. The gift that keeps on giving. SERVES 4 TO 6 TWICE

1 CHICKEN, 2 MEALS

Preheat your oven to 375°F (190°C). Turn on your convection fan if you have one.

Spread your vegetable selection in a large roasting pan. There should be enough to make a thick layer of flavor. Toss with a splash of oil if you like and season lightly with salt and pepper. Rub the chicken with a little oil if you like, and season well, inside and out. Perch it on top of the vegetables. Roast until the vegetables are tender and the chicken is deliciously golden brown, 2 hours or so. The chicken is juicy and safely done as soon as a thermometer inserted in the thick thigh reads 165°F (75°C).

Using two pairs of tongs or a pair of forks, pull and shred the meat from the bones, mixing it directly into the vegetables and juices below. As you free them, place the bones in a soup pot. Sprinkle the chicken and vegetables with green onions and fresh herbs. Serve and share!

Meanwhile, cover the chicken bones and scraps with 8 cups (2 L) or so of water. Toss in a bay leaf and bring the works to a slow, steady simmer. Cover and continue simmering, without stirring, until a rich, meaty broth forms, 2 hours or so. Strain and refrigerate for tomorrow's meal.

The next day when hunger strikes, simply reheat the broth along with all the leftovers from dinner. Toss in some frozen green peas, corn or edamame and season the soup with anything aromatic, including any fresh or dried herbs that strike your fancy.

FOR THE ROAST CHICKEN

3 to 4 pounds (1.35 to 1.8 kg) or
  so of onions, carrots, potatoes,
  sweet potatoes, apples or any root
  vegetables, coarsely chopped
A splash or two of olive oil (optional)
Salt and pepper
1 large roasting chicken (5 pounds/
  2.25 kg or so)
A few green onions, thinly sliced
A handful of your favorite fresh herb,
  chopped

FOR THE CHICKEN SOUP

A bay leaf
A cup or two (250 to 500 mL) of frozen
  green peas, corn or shelled edamame

FAMILY FLAVORS

A simple roast chicken is one of the bedrocks of home cooking. This particular method eliminates all the stress and strain of fussy carving while efficiently generating a second complete meal for your family.

IT'S EASY ENOUGH TO COOK GRAINS. IT'S JUST THAT THEY'RE NEVER READY WHEN YOU need them. The key is to keep a stash of precooked grains in your fridge—standby goodness ready to add to anything, anytime.

STIR-IN STUFF

FAMILY FLAVORS

You don't need a recipe to stir any of these into your meal. They're fair game for just about any salad, soup or stew. You can count on lots of flavor, texture and, perhaps most important, a jolt of tasty nutrition.

GRAIN	AMOUNT (UNCOOKED)	WATER	COOKING TIME	YIELD
Barley	1 cup (250 mL)	4 cups (1 L)	45 minutes	3½ cups (875 mL)
Bulgur	1 cup (250 mL)	2 cups (500 mL)	15 minutes	2½ cups (625 mL)
Millet	1 cup (250 mL)	2½ cups (625 mL)	20 minutes	3½ cups (875 mL)
Oats, old-fashioned rolled	1 cup (250 mL)	4 cups (1 L)	5 minutes	1¾ cups (425 mL)
Quinoa	1 cup (250 mL)	2 cups (500 mL)	15 minutes	3 cups (750 mL)
Rice, white	1 cup (250 mL)	2 cups (500 mL)	25 minutes	3 cups (750 mL)
Rice, brown long-grain	1 cup (250 mL)	2½ cups (625 mL)	40 minutes	3 cups (750 mL)
Rice, brown short-grain	1 cup (250 mL)	2 cups (500 mL)	45 minutes	3 cups (750 mL)
Rice, wild	1 cup (250 mL)	3 cups (750 mL)	45 minutes	3 cups (750 mL)
Rye berries	1 cup (250 mL)	3 cups (750 mL)	50 minutes	3 cups (750 mL)
Wheat berries	1 cup (250 mL)	3 cups (750 mL)	90 minutes	2½ cups (625 mL)

Measure the grain and water into a saucepan along with ½ teaspoon (2 mL) of salt. Bring to a slow, steady simmer, cover and continue simmering until the grain is tender and delicious, in about the time given. Turn off the heat and let rest for another 10 minutes or so before removing the lid. Refrigerate in a covered container until needed. They'll stay fresh for a week.

EVER WISHED YOU HAD A PERMANENT SALAD BAR AT HOME? THEN GO FOR IT! IT takes 2 minutes to shake together a tasty jar of your own salad dressing—real flavor, chemical-free. In another few minutes you can fill a few containers with ready-to-go prepped veggies, so anyone can toss together a salad at a moment's notice. Have fun together setting up the works, and watch as your family becomes regulars at their own all-you-can-eat salad bar! SERVES 4 TO 6 RIGHT AWAY OR AS NEEDED

YOUR HOUSE SALAD BAR

Craft the dressing easily by putting all the ingredients in a jar. Screw on the lid and give it a few good shakes until it's emulsified. Store in the refrigerator, and shake again before using.

You don't need a recipe for a great salad, just the desire to get 'er done. Find a bowl of any kind and fill it with greens, veggies and various assorted healthy crunchy bits. Pour on a few spoonfuls of dressing. Toss the works together, evenly mixing the flavors, textures and colors. Enjoy while you imagine how your next salad will be just as easy and just a little different.

FAMILY FLAVORS

Not all food is eaten at sit-down mealtimes, so a salad bar is a great way to offer your hungry hordes a healthy option for solo meals and snack times. It's all about convenience. Best of all, it doesn't take long to get the salad bar stocked and ready, or to replenish it midweek.

FOR THE DRESSING

½ cup (125 mL) or so of your very best olive oil

¼ cup (60 mL) or so of any vinegar

¼ cup (60 mL) of maple syrup, honey, brown sugar, jam, jelly or marmalade

A heaping spoonful of your favorite mustard

A heaping spoonful of any fresh or dried herb, spice, seasoning or condiment

FOR THE SALAD BAR IN YOUR FRIDGE

A good amount of any fresh mixed greens, baby spinach or arugula

A head or two of any lettuce (romaine, Bibb, leaf, radicchio, endive, frisée or iceberg), chopped or torn

Shredded carrots

Cherry tomatoes

Cauliflower or broccoli florets

Diced or sliced celery

Shredded or sliced radishes

Bean sprouts

Thinly sliced red or green onions

Cooked grains (see page 96)

Berries or grapes

THE TOPPINGS FROM YOUR PANTRY

Croutons

Nuts

Seeds

Dried fruits

Crushed tortilla chips

Canned chickpeas

FISHCAKES ARE A DELICIOUS WAY TO SLIP FISH PAST THE FINELY HONED DEFENSES of any finicky eaters at the table. They're also super simple to make and can easily spend a few days in the fridge waiting for dinner. Get ahead in advance so you can get ahead when it's time for dinner!

MAKES 8 FISHCAKES, SERVING 4

A MESS OF SMOKED SALMON FISHCAKES

FOR THE FISHCAKES

4 large baking potatoes, peeled and cubed

12 ounces (340 g) of any thinly sliced smoked salmon

2 green onions, thinly sliced

1 tablespoon (15 mL) of dried dill

1 tablespoon (15 mL) of prepared horseradish

1 teaspoon (5 mL) of salt

Lots of freshly ground pepper

2 eggs, beaten

FOR FRYING

¼ cup (60 mL) of all-purpose flour

1 tablespoon (15 mL) of vegetable oil

2 tablespoons (30 mL) of butter

Boil or steam the potatoes until they're tender, about 20 minutes. Mash the spuds while they're hot, then mix in the smoked salmon, breaking it up as you go. Stir in the green onions, dill, horseradish, salt and pepper. Let the works cool a bit before stirring in the eggs.

Shape the mixture into 8 fishcakes, each about an inch (2.5 cm) thick. Cover with plastic wrap and refrigerate for a few days, or if need be get right to frying.

Heat your favorite heavy skillet over medium-high heat. Dredge the fishcakes in the flour, shaking off the excess. Pour a puddle of oil into the pan and add a dollop of butter to the oil. (The butter will melt and flavor the works while the oil prevents the butter from burning. You'll get the best of both worlds.) Add the fishcakes, trying not to crowd the pan. Fry and sizzle, turning once, until golden brown and crispy, about 3 minutes per side. Serve and share!

FAMILY FLAVORS

You can easily double this recipe and stock your fridge or freezer with standby meals. You're not limited to smoked salmon, either. Any cooked fish will work well in the mix. Even a can or two of tuna is fair game!

Layer with parchment paper and freeze for a month or two in a tightly sealed freezer bag or wrapped tightly with plastic film.

THERE'S NOTHING GLAMOROUS ABOUT ALL THOSE ONE-OFF PIECES OF RIPE FRUIT that seem to accumulate in every kitchen. Rather than tossing them out, turn them into a tasty topping that is glamorous. A spoonful of this simple tasty stew instantly transforms pancakes, oatmeal, yogurt, a slice of cake or a simple bowl of ice cream into a special-occasion treat. MAKES 2 CUPS (500 ML) OR SO, EASILY DOUBLED OR TRIPLED

FRUIT STEW

Toss the fruit into a small saucepan along with the mint jelly and 2 tablespoons (30 mL) of fruit juice. Cook, stirring now and again, over medium-high heat just long enough for the works to come to a simmer, 5 minutes or so.

In a small bowl, stir the cornstarch into 1 teaspoon (5 mL) of fruit juice until dissolved. Stir the slurry into the simmering fruit, thickening the works almost immediately. Stir in the vanilla and lemon juice. Serve and share immediately or refrigerate to use throughout the week. The stew will keep for a week in your refrigerator and is best stored in a tightly sealed plastic container.

Try this fruit stew with these recipes:

- Nutty Seedy Granola, page 4
- Overnight Oatmeal Jars, page 8
- Weekend Pancakes, page 12
- Nutmeg Waffles, page 15
- French Toast, page 16

2 cups (500 mL) of bite-size pieces
  of any combination of ripe fruits
¼ cup (60 mL) of mint or
  raspberry jelly
2 tablespoons (30 mL) + 1 teaspoon
  (5 mL) of any fruit juice or water
1 teaspoon (5 mL) of cornstarch
¼ teaspoon (1 mL) of pure
  vanilla extract
A squeeze or two of lemon juice

FAMILY FLAVORS

Keep an ever-growing stash of different ripe fruits in your freezer until you have enough to trigger making a batch of this stew. Just thaw the works in the fridge overnight and carry on.

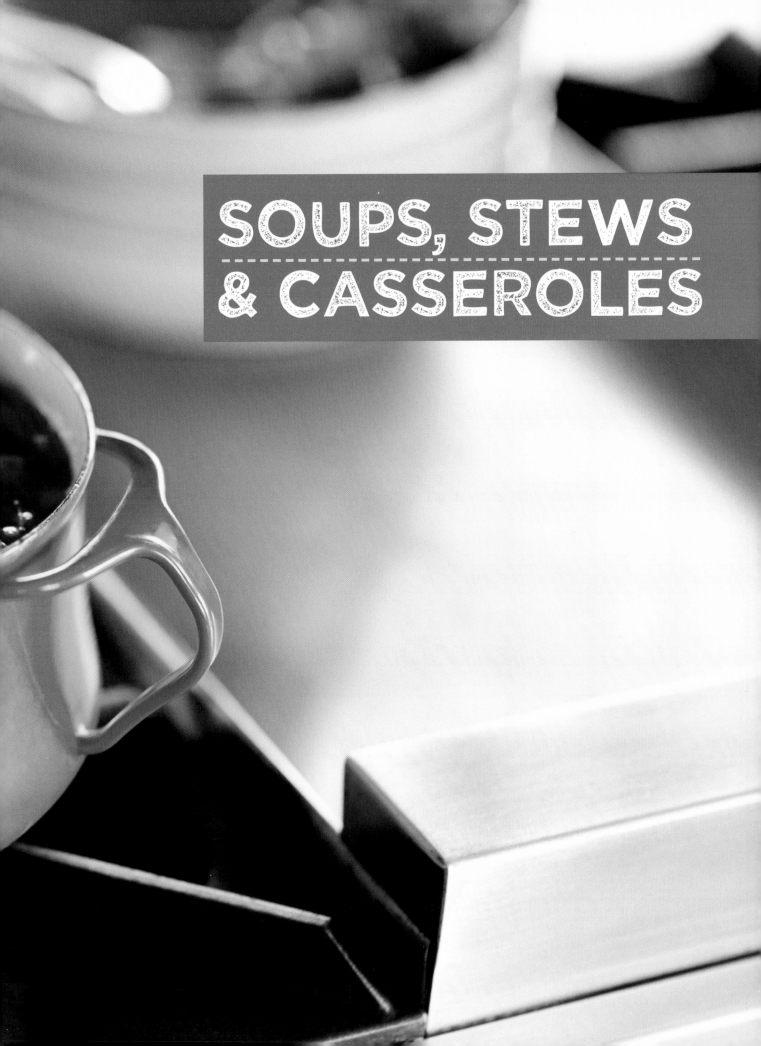

SOUPS, STEWS & CASSEROLES

FAMILY RECIPES

THERE ARE AS MANY SOUPS AS THERE ARE COOKS, POTS AND VEGETABLES, AND JUST as many reasons to take the time to craft your own. Time-honored puréed soups are a super-simple way to get a whole lot of vegetable flavor on the table in a hurry (and to hide vegetables from those who aren't crazy about them). You just might end up discovering a table full of vegetable lovers. Start by treating yourself to a hand blender. MAKES 4 HEARTY BOWLS OF HOMEMADE GOODNESS

PURÉED VEGETABLE SOUP 101

YOUR CHOICE OF VEGETABLE AND ACCOMPANYING AROMATIC FLAVORS— MIX AND MATCH!

2 tablespoons (30 mL) of butter, more if you're feeling indulgent, even a lot more, up to ½ cup (125 mL)

A large onion or two, finely chopped

2 or 3 or 8 garlic cloves, thinly sliced

4 cups (1 L) of chicken or vegetable broth (or just plain water, which works fine)

1 teaspoon (5 mL) of salt

Lots of freshly ground pepper

CHOOSE A VEGETABLE FLAVOR ...	... AND ITS FLAVOR PARTNER.
6 red bell peppers	1 tablespoon (15 mL) of fennel seeds
1 can of any beans, drained and rinsed	Zest and juice of 1 lemon
1 pound (450 g) or so of carrots	1 tablespoon (15 mL) of ground cumin
1 big head of broccoli	½ teaspoon (2 mL) of nutmeg
1 turnip	1 tablespoon (15 mL) of fresh thyme
2 sweet potatoes	1 tablespoon (15 mL) of cinnamon
1 head of cauliflower	1 tablespoon (15 mL) of curry powder
2 pounds (900 g) of mushrooms	1 tablespoon (15 mL) of chopped fresh rosemary
6 cups (1.5 L) of green peas	1 bunch of mint + 1 teaspoon (5 mL) more salt
2 large bunches of kale, center stems removed	1 whole head of garlic, minced

FAMILY FLAVORS

Soups are the workhorses of professional kitchens, because they're the easiest way to make a lot of food in a hurry. Personalize them for your family. Add crunch with nuts, seeds or crumbled crackers. Stir in thinly sliced deli meat, crisp bacon or any cheese, grated or crumbled. Or how about salsa, pesto, tapenade? You name it. You can stir anything into these soups and call them your own.

Choose your vegetable and its flavor partner. Grate hard vegetables, and cut others into small pieces.

In a soup pot, melt the butter over medium-high heat. Toss in the onions and garlic, stirring as the onions soften. Keep the heat high enough to sizzle but not high enough to scorch. Add your chosen vegetable and pour in the broth. Bring to a slow, steady simmer. Simmer, stirring occasionally, brightening the flavors, 20 minutes or so—just long enough for the vegetables to soften but not long enough for the flavors to peak and fade. In the last minute or two, stir in your chosen flavor partner. Season with salt and pepper.

Purée the works using your hand blender, tilting the pot and going for the depths. Keep going until you've reached soup thickness. Go further for smoother. Holler, ladle, serve and share!

CHICKEN SOUP IS UNIVERSAL. ALL OVER THE WORLD, YARD BIRDS END UP IN THE communal pot along with lots of local flavors and stories. Your bowlful of these slurpy noodles is just the latest from a long line of global soup pots. SERVES 4 TO 6

ASIAN CHICKEN NOODLE SOUP

Begin the chicken broth: Throw the chicken pieces into a soup pot and cover with the water. Too easy! Add the flavorful onions, garlic and ginger. Bring to a slow, steady simmer over increasingly lower heat. Cover and very gently simmer for an hour or so as the gentle heat tenderizes the meat, extracting richness and flavor from the flesh and bones.

One by one, fish out the chicken pieces, ease out the bones, throw them out, pull the meat into bite-size pieces if need be, and return the meaty proceeds to the pot. Add the carrot, green onions, greens, udon noodles, soy sauce, ginger and vinegar. Bring to a slow, steady simmer. By now you're hungry, so cook just long enough for the flavors to brighten and the textures to soften, 10 minutes or so. Ladle into bowls, top with some cilantro, serve, share and slurp!

FAMILY FLAVORS

There's more than one way to get the flavor out of fresh ginger and more than one way for a family to find those foodways that stand the test of time, the tricks and techniques that transcend the kitchen and become family legend. Maybe grating frozen ginger will become your family's. It's that good a trick!

This soup is perfect for the lunchbox too. It's easily reheated and just as delicious tomorrow.

FOR THE BASIC CHICKEN BROTH

3 pounds (1.35 kg) or so of chicken wings, drumsticks, thighs or whole legs
16 cups (3.8 L) of water
2 onions, thinly sliced
Cloves from 1 head of garlic, thinly sliced
2 inches (5 cm) or so of frozen ginger, grated

TO TRANSFORM THE BROTH INTO SOUP

1 carrot, cut into ribbons with a vegetable peeler
2 bunches of green onions, thinly sliced
8 ounces (225 g) of any Asian greens (bok choy, lo choy, etc.), chopped
1 pound (450 g) of fresh udon noodles
6 tablespoons (90 mL) of soy sauce
2 inches (5 cm) of frozen ginger, grated
2 tablespoons (30 mL) of rice wine vinegar
A handful of tender fresh cilantro

IN THE MARITIMES, EVERY FAMILY HAS THEIR OWN CHOWDER RECIPE, A TRADITIONAL feed passed down through generations of kitchens, from fisher folk and those who fed them. This is my family's chowder. It's full of our flavors and stories, and we hope you enjoy it. SERVES 4 TO 6

MARITIME MUSSEL CHOWDER

4 slices of bacon, chopped

1 or 2 onions, chopped

2 celery ribs, chopped

A few cloves of garlic, thinly sliced

A generous splash of any white wine

1 cup (250 mL) of whipping cream

1 cup (250 mL) of water

5 pounds (2.25 kg) of fresh mussels, scrubbed, debearded and rinsed well

2 bay leaves

A handful of fresh thyme sprigs, half whole, half finely chopped

2 large Prince Edward Island potatoes (unpeeled), diced

A 12-ounce (375 mL) can of unsweetened evaporated milk

A handful of fresh parsley leaves, chopped

Lots of freshly ground pepper

Toss the bacon into your soup pot. Pour in ½ cup (125 mL) of water (this helps the bacon cook evenly). Set the heat to medium-high and cook, stirring often, until the water is evaporated and the bacon is crisp, 10 minutes or so.

Add the onions, celery and garlic. Continue cooking and stirring as the flavors deepen and textures soften, 2 or 3 minutes. Splash in the wine, then add the cream and water. Pour in the mussels, then add the bay leaves and the whole thyme sprigs. Bring to a vigorous boil for a moment, then immediately reduce the heat to a slow, steady simmer and cover. Cook for 10 minutes. Remove from the heat.

Pitch any mussels that haven't opened. Fish out the delicious little nuggets of mussel meat, letting the broth trickle back into the pot. Put the mussels in a bowl and discard the shells.

Return the pot to a slow, steady simmer. Toss in the potatoes and simmer until they soften and release their starches, partially thickening the surrounding broth into chowder, 20 minutes or so. Finish the chowder with the delicate evaporated milk, the reserved mussel meat, the chopped thyme, the parsley and pepper. Serve and share with your favorite biscuits!

FAMILY FLAVORS

Ladies and gentlemen, welcome to today's Chowder Cup! In this corner, Team Chowder, ready to slice, dice, stir and slurp their way to the finish line with this recipe. On this side, the Bakers, with their death-defying speedy biscuits. Who will reach the table first? Who will take the flavor lead? There's nothing like turning dinner into a family-fun rally! The reward? A bowl of chowder, a biscuit or two and dinner together.

A BAG OF FRESH PRINCE EDWARD ISLAND MUSSELS—THE WORLD'S EASIEST-TO-COOK seafood—and a can of tomatoes are the simple foundations of this delicious supper. Fresh mussels always deliver two things: tasty morsels of meat and a pot full of tasty broth. Throw in a few flavors and flourishes, and before you know it you'll be enjoying a hearty bowl of the deep! SERVES 4, MAYBE 6

TOMATO CAN MUSSEL SOUP

Splash the oil into your soup pot over medium-high heat. Add the onions and garlic. Cook, stirring, as the onions soften, 2 or 3 minutes. Splash in the wine, pour in the tomatoes and stir in the oregano. Season with a few turns of your pepper grinder. Tumble the mussels on top of the works. Bring everything to a vigorous boil for a moment, then immediately reduce the heat to a slow, steady simmer and cover. Cook for 10 minutes. Remove from the heat.

Pitch any mussels that haven't opened. Working over the pot, fish out the delicious little nuggets of mussel meat, letting the meat and the broth fall back into the pot and discarding the shells. Stir in the parsley and green onions. Brighten with the lemon. Simmer to heat through, then serve and share!

2 tablespoons (30 mL) of vegetable oil

1 or 2 large onions, thinly sliced

6 to 8 garlic cloves, thinly sliced

1 cup (250 mL) of your favorite red or white wine

A 28-ounce (796 mL) can of crushed, puréed or diced tomatoes

1 or 2 teaspoons (5 or 10 mL) of dried oregano

Freshly ground pepper

5 pounds (2.25 kg) of fresh mussels, scrubbed, debearded and rinsed well

A big handful of fresh parsley, chopped

2 or 3 green onions, thinly sliced

The zest and juice of 1 lemon

FAMILY FLAVORS

Parenting sometimes involves wine, so there may be a bottle to pour from. No matter the type, it will add depth and balance to the tomatoes. Tell yourself the soup comes first, and open a bottle of your favorite and pour a cup into the mussel pot. What happens to the rest is up to you.

SOMETIMES IT TAKES GOOD PUBLIC RELATIONS AND MARKETING TO SELL A HEALTHY dinner to your kids. That's what this soup is all about. The name alone sells any tentative taster, and once they dive in to the familiar fun flavors, they'll never notice it's really a bowl of homemade goodness.
SERVES 4 TO 6

PIZZA SOUP

FOR THE SOUP POT

2 tablespoons (30 mL) of olive oil

2 onions, chopped

6 to 8 garlic cloves, minced

A 28-ounce (796 mL) can of
    crushed tomatoes

1 tablespoon (15 mL) of dried oregano

3 cups (750 mL) or so of your favorite
    pizza toppings (such as sliced
    bell peppers, mushrooms, olives,
    cooked bacon)

4 ounces (115 g) of spicy pepperoni,
    thinly sliced into rounds and halved

4 cups (1 L) of rich chicken broth or
    plain old water

½ teaspoon (2 mL) of salt (but none if
    you use store-bought chicken broth)

Lots of freshly ground pepper

FOR THE OVENPROOF SOUP BOWLS

4 to 6 slices of your favorite
    multigrain bread

8 to 12 ounces (225 to 340 g)
    of shredded mozzarella or pizza-
    blend cheese

Preheat your broiler.

Splash the olive oil into your soup pot over medium-high heat. Add the onions and garlic. Cook, stirring, as the onions soften, 2 or 3 minutes. Pour in the tomatoes, then stir in the oregano, your pizza toppings and the pepperoni. Pour in the chicken broth and season with salt and pepper. Bring to a vigorous boil for a moment, then immediately reduce the heat to a slow, steady simmer and cover. Cook, stirring occasionally, until the flavors brighten and the textures soften, 10 minutes or so.

While the soup simmers, toast the bread, then trim it to fit into ovenproof soup bowls. Set the toasts aside and put the bowls on a baking sheet. Ladle the soup into the bowls. Top each with a slice of toast. Add a thick topping of cheese, then broil until the cheese deliciously melts and browns, 5 minutes or so. Keep an eye on the works, moving or turning the tray as needed for even browning. Serve and share!

FAMILY FLAVORS

The flavors of pizza are great no matter how you mix them up, and this inspired soup contains them all. The oregano in particular defines the iconic flavor.

A HEARTY BOWL OF BEEF STEW IS ONE OF THE MOST VERSATILE DISHES OF ANY kitchen. You can prepare it for an easy weekday supper or add a few flourishes along the way for a special weekend dinner. As always, the secret ingredient is patience. There's simply no substitute for patient browning and simmering. Serve with a basket of freshly baked biscuits. SERVES 4 TO 6

WEEKNIGHT OR WEEKEND BEEF STEW

Heat your largest, heaviest pot over medium-high heat while you gently dry the beef on a few paper towels. Splash a pool of oil into the pot, swirling and covering the bottom with a thin film. Using tongs, carefully add a single sizzling layer of beef without crowding the pan. This is your only shot at adding the rich, deep flavors that can only come from respectfully browned meat. Listen to the heat. A simmering pan means nothing. Sizzle is the sound of flavor. Too loud, though, and a sizzling pan becomes a smoking-burning pan. When the beef is deeply browned all over, transfer it to a plate. Repeat with the rest of the beef, 10 to 15 minutes in total. Pour off any excess oil, leaving behind any browned bits of goodness.

Add the onions, carrots, celery, potatoes, tomatoes, wine, broth, bay leaves, salt and pepper. Return all the beef to the pot. Stirring frequently, bring to a furious full boil, then immediately reduce the heat to a slow, steady simmer. Cover tightly and very gently simmer for at least an hour, another if you can, stirring now and then, patiently tenderizing the meat, releasing the richness and building deep beefy flavor.

The stew is hearty and satisfying as is, so go ahead and serve and share right away. It does benefit from a dash of last-second flavor, though, so if you like, toss in—or top with—your chosen finishing flavors.

FAMILY FLAVORS

Years from now your kids and friends will vividly remember the bowls of beef stew they enjoyed at your table. This iconic dish is woven into the very fabric of our being. Humans have been browning meat since flames were harnessed. We instinctively crave the deep, rich flavors of browned beef and will remember on a primal level where we enjoyed it.

FOR THE CLASSIC WEEKNIGHT STEW

2 pounds (900 g) of cubed
   stewing beef

2 tablespoons (30 mL) of vegetable oil

2 onions, chopped

2 carrots, chopped

2 celery ribs, chopped

2 potatoes (or 2 or 3 parsnips
   or 2 sweet potatoes or a turnip),
   chopped

A 28-ounce (796 mL) can of whole,
   diced, crushed or puréed tomatoes

1 bottle of big, beefy red wine (pour
   some for the grown-ups first!)

4 cups (1 L) of beef broth or plain water

2 bay leaves

1 tablespoon (15 mL) of sea salt

Lots of freshly ground pepper

WEEKEND FINISHING FLOURISHES—CHOOSE 1 OR 2 OR ALL

4 green onions, thinly sliced

Leaves from 1 bunch of fresh thyme,
   sage, tarragon or rosemary, minced

1 to 2 cups (250 to 500 mL) of frozen
   green peas

1 bunch of asparagus, trimmed
   and chopped

A 14-ounce (398 mL) can of chickpeas,
   drained and rinsed

8 slices of bacon, cooked crisp
   and crumbled

1 wheel (5.2 ounces/150 g) of your
   favorite Boursin cheese, crumbled

FEW DISHES ARE AS DELICIOUS AS AN OLD-FASHIONED PAN OF CREAMED CHICKEN stew topped with tender dumplings. It's the sort of centerpiece dish that can spark a riot at your table. But you don't have to roast a whole chicken like Grandma did to excite the crowd. Speed things up with just a pair of standard-issue chicken breasts. SERVES 4

STOVETOP CHICKEN WITH HERB DUMPLINGS

FOR THE CREAMY CHICKEN STEW

1 tablespoon (15 mL) of vegetable oil

1 tablespoon (15 mL) or so of butter

2 boneless, skinless chicken breasts

1 large onion, chopped

2 celery ribs, diced

1 large carrot, diced

4 garlic cloves, thinly sliced

2 tablespoons (30 mL) of all-purpose
    flour

1 cup (250 mL) of white wine

1 cup (250 mL) of whipping cream

1 cup (250 mL) of water

1 cup (250 mL) of frozen green peas
    or corn

1 tablespoon (15 mL) of fresh thyme

1 teaspoon (5 mL) of salt

Lots of freshly ground pepper

FOR THE TENDER DUMPLINGS

1 cup (250 mL) of all-purpose flour

2 teaspoons (10 mL) of baking powder

½ teaspoon (2 mL) of white sugar

½ teaspoon (2 mL) of salt

A handful of chopped fresh parsley
    (or 2 green onions, thinly sliced)

½ cup (125 mL) of milk

¼ cup (60 mL) of butter, melted

Start making the stew. Heat your favorite heavy skillet over medium-high heat. Pour in the vegetable oil, then add the butter (the oil prevents the butter from burning). Add and sear the chicken breasts, building a golden-brown crispy crust on each side, about 15 minutes total. Remove the delicious chicken to a plate.

To the skillet, add the onions, celery, carrot and garlic along with a splash or two of water to loosen and dissolve all the flavorful browned bits. Stir and cook until sizzling, 5 minutes or so. Reduce the heat to medium. Sprinkle in the flour and stir until it's evenly absorbed by the butter. Pour in the wine and stir the works again. Pour in the cream and water and continue cooking, stirring often, until the sauce is beautifully thickened and smooth.

Meanwhile, chop the chicken into bite-size pieces. Return them to the pan along with the peas. Season with thyme, salt and pepper. Turn off the heat.

To make the dumplings, in a medium bowl, whisk together the flour, baking powder, sugar and salt. Stir in the parsley. Add the milk and melted butter, and stir together until the dough is just blended. Return the chicken stew to a slow simmer. Spoon 10 or 12 dumplings over the stew. Cook, uncovered, for 10 minutes, then cover tightly and cook until the dumplings are fluffy and tender, about 10 more minutes. Spoon, serve and share!

FAMILY FLAVORS

Sometimes life needs a dish like this, waiting warmly and patiently as a family comes together to share at the table. That's a lot of pressure for a simple recipe, but this one's up to it.

THIS IS AN EXTRAORDINARY WAY TO ELEVATE A HUMBLE CHICKEN WITH TWO BASIC starting points: the reliably sunny flavors of traditional Greek cooking and a simple cooking method that's stood the test of time. No mythology here, though. Just addictive flavor. THIS IS HOW YOU STRETCH A CHICKEN TO SERVE UP TO 8 HUNGRY MOUTHS ...

GREEK CHICKEN

Preheat your oven to 350°F (180°C).

Toss the potatoes with oil and spread evenly in your roasting pan. Using a serrated knife, trim the top third off each head of garlic, exposing the cloves within. Nestle the garlic heads cut side up into the corners of the roasting pan. Zest the lemons, reserving the zest, and cut the lemons in half. Stuff them into the chicken along with the whole oregano sprigs. Season the chicken and the potatoes with salt and pepper. Pour the water into the pan. Place the chicken on the potatoes and into the oven.

Roast for 2 hours or so, until the potatoes are tender and the chicken is deliciously golden brown. A thermometer inserted in the thick thigh should read at least 165°F (75°C).

Remove the chicken to a plate to rest for a few minutes. Carefully squeeze the soft garlic heads over the roasted potatoes. Sprinkle with the chopped oregano and reserved lemon zest, and stir in the green onions. Pour any juices from the chicken plate over the works and rest the bird on the spuds while you carve, serve and share!

6 to 8 large baking potatoes, each cut into 8 wedges (enough to fill your roasting pan)

2 tablespoons (30 mL) of olive oil

4 heads of garlic

2 lemons

1 large roasting chicken (5 pounds/ 2.25 kg or so)

1 big bunch of fresh oregano, half whole, half chopped

1 teaspoon (5 mL) of salt

Lots of freshly ground pepper

1 cup (250 mL) of water

4 green onions, thinly sliced

FAMILY FLAVORS

Every cook needs to stretch a chicken into dinner for the masses now and then. To best manage portion control, leave the chicken right where it is and carve the meat over the potatoes, cutting, tugging and pulling the meat from the bones, removing and discarding the bones (or saving them to make a simple broth).

THIS IS A GREAT DISH FOR TAKE-OUT OR EAT-IN. IT'S PACKED WITH FAMILIAR FLAVORS, easy to get into the oven and even easier to walk away from. Be patient, though. Although it's ready in 2 hours, it's even better after 3. SERVES 4 TO 6, AND DON'T COUNT ON LEFTOVERS

SLOW-BAKED CHICKEN LEGS WITH BARBECUE FLAVORS

A 19-ounce (540 mL) can of diced, crushed or whole tomatoes

½ cup (125 mL) of your favorite barbecue sauce

2 tablespoons (30 mL) of red, white or cider vinegar

2 tablespoons (30 mL) of molasses

2 tablespoons (30 mL) of yellow mustard

1 tablespoon (15 mL) of ground cumin

1 tablespoon (15 mL) of chili powder

1 teaspoon (5 mL) of salt

2 cans (28 ounces/796 mL each) of red or black beans, drained and rinsed

2 red bell peppers, cut into eighths

At least 4 peeled garlic cloves, maybe a few more

6 chicken legs (or 12 thighs, or 12 drumsticks, or your custom blend)

4 green onions, thinly sliced

A handful of fresh cilantro sprigs

2 limes, cut into 8 wedges

Preheat your oven to 325°F (160°C). Turn on your convection fan if you have one. Get out your favorite heavy covered casserole dish. Make sure the chicken will fit in it in a single layer. Alternatively, use a roasting pan and cover tightly with foil when the time comes.

Splash, pour, measure and sprinkle in the tomatoes, barbecue sauce, vinegar, molasses, mustard, cumin, chili powder and salt. Stir well. Stir in the beans, red peppers and garlic cloves. Nestle in the chicken legs. Cover and put in the oven. Walk away and live a little for about 2 hours, 3 if you're patient and like more browning. The chicken will become tender and flavorful. You'll know it's done when you can easily slip out the bones.

Serve and share on a festive platter, casually sprinkled with green onions and cilantro sprigs, with lime wedges tucked in at the sides.

FAMILY FLAVORS
- - - - - - - - - - -
Life rewards patience. It's pretty easy to pile a gang of flavors into a pot and do nothing while your oven does everything. The trade-off is time—at least 2 hours, better 3 for this dish—but that time is also the secret to great flavor. You can get a lot done while dinner's cooking and you just know everyone's going to love it!

I LEARNED A FEW KITCHEN TRICKS IN MOROCCO. THINGS LIKE HOW WELL CINNAMON and cumin go together. How much time you save when you don't brown the meat for a stew. How every dish there seems to have lots of spices, citrus, nuts and dried fruits, and more. Most of all I learned how global the quest for flavor is! SERVES 4 TO 6, WITH LEFTOVERS

MOROCCAN-STYLE CINNAMON CUMIN LAMB

Place your favorite stew pot over medium-high heat. Add the lamb, tomatoes, orange juice, onions, carrots, garlic, marmalade, cumin and cinnamon, stirring and submerging the meat in aromatic flavor. Stirring frequently, bring the works to a furious boil, then immediately reduce the heat to a slow, steady simmer. Cover tightly and very gently simmer for 90 minutes, stirring now and then, patiently forming the aromatic sauce, tenderizing the meat, releasing the richness and building bright flavor.

In the last few minutes of cooking, stir in the chickpeas, cumin, cinnamon, hot sauce and lemon zest and juice. Simmer gently to heat through. (The additional cumin and cinnamon will brighten the flavors.) Sprinkle the nuts and fruit on as finishing garnish. Strew cilantro sprigs over top, serve and share!

FAMILY FLAVORS

- - - - - - - - - -

A great place to engage your kids is in the kitchen—and at the table. Preparing a dish from another culture can be a fascinating lesson in the ways of the world. The dish's flavors may be different than what you're used to, but at heart it's still just food—and we all have to eat!

FOR THE STEW

1 boneless leg of lamb (2½ to 3 pounds/1.125 to 1.35 kg), cubed

A 28-ounce (796 mL) can of diced or whole tomatoes

2 cups (500 mL) of orange juice

2 onions, peeled and cut into eighths

2 carrots, thinly sliced

Cloves from 1 head of garlic

½ cup (125 mL) of marmalade

1 tablespoon (15 mL) of ground cumin

1 tablespoon (15 mL) of cinnamon

FOR THE FINISH AND FLOURISH

A 19-ounce (540 mL) can of chickpeas, drained and rinsed

1 teaspoon (5 mL) of ground cumin

1 teaspoon (5 mL) of cinnamon

½ teaspoon (2 mL) of your favorite hot sauce

The zest and juice of 1 lemon

1 cup (250 mL) of pistachios, pine nuts or slivered almonds

1 cup (250 mL) of plump raisins, sliced dried apricots or sliced pitted dates

A handful of fresh cilantro sprigs

SLOW COOKERS
& PRESSURE COOKERS

FAMILY RECIPES

YOU CAN DO A LOT OF THINGS IN YOUR SLOW COOKER—IT CAN BE A REAL LIFESAVER. Here it slowly transforms some quickly gathered ingredients into a deeply flavored, satisfying lasagna just waiting for the family to get home. SERVES 4 TO 6, WITH SECONDS AND LEFTOVERS

ALL-DAY SAUSAGE LASAGNA

1 tablespoon (15 mL) of vegetable oil

4 spicy Italian sausages, thickly sliced

1 large onion, chopped

8 garlic cloves, thinly sliced

A 28-ounce (796 mL) can of
crushed tomatoes

A 5.5-ounce (156 mL) can of
tomato paste

2 tablespoons (30 mL) of
dried oregano

4 cups (1 L) or so of shredded
mozzarella (about 10 ounces/280 g)

12 ounces (340 g) of cottage cheese

½ cup (125 mL) of freshly grated
Parmigiano-Reggiano

8 ounces (225 g) or so of oven-ready
lasagna noodles (12 to 14 noodles)

Preheat your favorite heavy skillet over medium-high heat. Pour in the vegetable oil and toss in the sausages, searing until browned all over, about 10 minutes. Add the onions and garlic and continue sautéing as the onions soften, 2 or 3 more minutes. Stir in the tomatoes, tomato paste and oregano. Remove from the heat.

Fill your slow cooker with layers of flavor. Begin with one-third of the sausage mixture, then follow with one-third of the two cheeses, half the noodles, a third of the sausage, a third of the cheeses, the remaining noodles, the remaining sausage mixture and the remaining cheese. Cover and cook on low for 4 to 6 hours. When you get back from wherever life takes you, serve and share!

FAMILY FLAVORS

Kids love this lasagna. They gobble it up and always ask for seconds! This is an easy dish to tote along to a potluck party. The slow cooker cooks the dish and also serves as a warming holder.

A SLOW COOKER WILL HELP YOU PULL OFF THIS MEAL ON A BUSY WEEKNIGHT. TO speed things up, schedule a little meatball rally after dinner the night before, so in the morning you can just pop the works into the slow cooker and go get your day. When you come home, all you have to do is boil the spaghetti and get to slurping! SERVES 4 TO 6, WITH SOME SECONDS

SPAGHETTI AND MEATBALLS AND SAUSAGE

Whip up the meatballs first and have them waiting in the slow cooker for the equally speedy sauce. Simply toss the ground beef into a bowl along with the remaining meatball ingredients. Use your hands to mix the works thoroughly, evenly distributing the flavors and textures. Form into at least 12 small balls and place directly in the slow cooker. Top with the sausages.

Now make the sauce. Splash the olive oil into your favorite large saucepan over medium-high heat. Toss in the onions and garlic and sauté for a few minutes, building flavor. Pour in the crushed tomatoes, diced tomatoes and tomato paste, then stir in the bay leaf, salt and pepper. Bring to a furious boil, then pour the sauce over the meatballs and sausages. Cover and cook on low for 8 hours. Ten minutes before it's done, boil the spaghetti. Serve and share!

FAMILY FLAVORS

Kids love this classic; they pile up their plates and go back for more. It's an easy dish to tote along to a pot-luck party too.

When time is of the essence, you can adjust your cooking expectations. For instance, you don't always need the deep flavors of caramelization. You save time by not browning the meatballs and sausages, but you lose roasted flavor. No worries. Time is on your side, and with it, the satisfying flavors that emerge from a slow cooker.

FOR THE MEATBALLS

1 pound (450 g) of fatty ground beef

1 large onion, grated on the large holes of a box grater

4 garlic cloves, minced

½ cup (125 mL) of freshly grated Parmigiano-Reggiano cheese

1 egg, lightly beaten

A handful of minced fresh parsley

1 tablespoon (15 mL) of dried oregano

1 teaspoon (5 mL) of nutmeg

½ teaspoon (2 mL) of sea salt

Lots of freshly ground pepper

FOR THE SAUCE

2 tablespoons (30 mL) of olive oil

2 large onions, sliced

Cloves from 1 head of garlic, sliced

A 28-ounce (796 mL) can of crushed tomatoes

A 28-ounce (796 mL) can of diced tomatoes

A 5.5-ounce (156 mL) can of tomato paste

1 bay leaf

½ tsp (2 mL) of sea salt

Lots of freshly ground pepper

THE OTHER THINGS YOU'LL NEED

4 Italian sausages, sliced into 1-inch (2.5 cm) rounds

1 pound (450 g) of spaghetti

THESE CLASSIC FLAVORS HAVE STOOD THE TEST OF TIME. SOAK THE BEANS overnight, or use the quick-soak method in the early morning. Either way, your slow cooker is perfect for coaxing maximum tenderness out of the beans and putting max flavor in. SERVES 4 TO 6, WITH SECONDS AND LEFTOVERS

BACON BAKED BEANS

3 cups (750 mL) of dried white beans

8 slices of bacon, diced

1 large onion, chopped

A 5.5-ounce (156 mL) can of
   tomato paste

1 cup (250 mL) of molasses

1 cup (250 mL) of yellow mustard

2 teaspoons (10 mL) of your favorite
   hot sauce

3 cups (750 mL) of water

FAMILY FLAVORS

It's not what's on the table, it's who's at the table that really matters. Food is for gathering, preparing and sharing, each step as important as the others. It's important that the food be honest and delicious, but ultimately it's your family's time spent together that's the real star of the show.

The only hard part about cooking beans is remembering to soak them the day before you need them. Simply toss them into a bowl and cover generously with water. Let sit overnight. The beans will slowly absorb water and begin to soften, making them much easier to cook. When you're ready to get cooking, drain and rinse them. (Alternatively, quick-soak your beans. Toss them into a pot, cover with lots of water and bring to a furious boil for a few minutes. Turn off the heat, cover tightly and let sit for 1 hour. Drain and rinse.)

Toss the bacon into a heavy skillet. Add 1 cup (250 mL) of water (this helps the bacon cook evenly). Set the heat to medium-high and cook, stirring often, until the water is evaporated and the bacon is crisp, 10 minutes or so. Pour off about half of the flavorful fat to lighten things up. Or not.

Pour the bacon and its fat into the slow cooker. Add the onions, tomato paste, molasses, mustard, hot sauce, drained beans and the water. Give everything a good stir. Cover and cook on low for 8 hours or so. Serve with crusty bread and share with your favorite people!

YOUR SLOW COOKER IS ONE OF THE MOST VERSATILE AND EASY-TO-USE TOOLS IN your kitchen. It can transform a big beef pot roast into the French regional dish of your choice—Alsatian, Bordeaux or Provençale. Fix it and forget it! SERVES 4 TO 6

TRIO OF FRENCH POT ROASTS

For each pot roast, your path is the same. Put everything but the beef in the slow cooker (if you're making the Provençale dish, hold back the olives and capers till the end) and give it a good stir. Nestle the meat into the works. Cover and cook on low for 8 hours or more or on high for 6 hours or so. Turn once or twice if you can, no worries if you can't.

For the Provençale pot roast, stir in the olives and capers at the end. Serve, share and toast your success with a glass of wine from your chosen French appellation!

FAMILY FLAVORS

Go on a vacation without leaving your kitchen! Wherever you end up, you'll discover what cooks all over the world know: slowly, patiently simmering meat always makes it tender.

FOR THE HEARTY NORTHERN FLAVORS OF ALSACE

2 cups (500 mL) of Alsatian or any red wine

½ cup (125 mL) of brown sugar

¼ cup (60 mL) of red wine vinegar

2 tablespoons (30 mL) of grainy mustard

1 tablespoon (15 mL) of fennel seeds

1 tablespoon (15 mL) of caraway seeds

1 teaspoon (5 mL) of ground allspice

1 teaspoon (5 mL) of salt

1 teaspoon (5 mL) of your favorite hot sauce

1 head of red cabbage, thinly sliced

1 big beef pot roast (3 pounds/1.35 kg or so), cut in half

FOR THE RUSTIC FLAVORS OF BORDEAUX

1 bottle of big, beefy Bordeaux or your favorite red wine

1 large onion, chopped

6 to 8 garlic cloves, halved

2 pounds (900 g) of 2 or 3 different mushrooms, sliced

1½ pounds (675 g) of baby potatoes (or 4 baking potatoes, each cut into 8 chunks)

1 tablespoon (15 mL) of dried thyme

2 teaspoons (10 mL) of salt

2 bay leaves

1 big beef pot roast (3 pounds/1.35 kg or so), cut in half

FOR THE BRIGHT, SUNNY FLAVORS OF PROVENCE

2 large onions, chopped

Cloves from 1 head of garlic, peeled

A 28-ounce (796 mL) can of diced tomatoes

A 14-ounce (398 mL) can of chickpeas, drained and rinsed

1 tablespoon (15 mL) of dried oregano

1 tablespoon (15 mL) of red wine vinegar

1 teaspoon (5 mL) of salt

1 big beef pot roast (3 pounds/1.35 kg or so), cut in half

1 cup (250 mL) of pitted black olives

2 tablespoons (30 mL) of capers

MY BUDDY CHEF JESSE VERGEN DISHES BBQ OUT OF A CABOOSE CALLED THE Smoking Pig, in Quispamsis, New Brunswick. He's got a rolling smoke house parked next to the works and pushes beef brisket, pork shoulders and various slow-smoked local fowl out the back window. With a lot of sauce. I staked out the joint and caught him pouring root beer into his house sauce. SERVES A CROWD OF 8 TO 12 CARNIVORES

CABOOSE-STYLE PULLED PORK WITH HONEY MUSTARD SLAW

FOR THE BARBECUE FLAVORS

1 pork shoulder or butt (3 pounds/
  1.35 kg or so)
1 tablespoon (15 mL) of chili powder
1 tablespoon (15 mL) of ground cumin
1 tablespoon (15 mL) of paprika
1 tablespoon (15 mL) of garlic powder
1 tablespoon (15 mL) of onion powder
1 tablespoon (15 mL) of dried oregano
¼ cup (60 mL) of molasses (or honey
  or brown sugar)
¼ cup (60 mL) of Dijon mustard
1 bottle (355 mL) of local root
  beer, such as J.J. Stewart or
  Babbling Brooke's
½ cup (125 mL) of cider vinegar
½ teaspoon (2 mL) or more of your
  favorite hot sauce

FOR THE SNAPPY COLESLAW

2 tablespoons (30 mL) of honey
2 tablespoons (30 mL) of
  yellow mustard
2 tablespoons (30 mL) of cider vinegar
1 tablespoon (15 mL) of olive oil
½ teaspoon (2 mL) of sea salt
½ teaspoon (2 mL) of your favorite
  hot sauce
1 bag (about 14 ounces/400 g) of
  coleslaw mix (or 4 cups/1 L of
  shredded cabbages and carrots)

FOR THE SANDWICHES

8 to 12 of your favorite crusty sandwich
  rolls or buns, split and warmed

Some morning preheat your slow cooker at its lowest setting.

Cut the pork shoulder into 4 pieces and snuggle them into their home for the day. Whisk the dry spices together in a medium bowl. Set aside half of the mixture, then stir the molasses, mustard, root beer, vinegar and hot sauce into the rest. Pour the works over the meat, flipping the pieces to evenly distribute the flavors. Cover and walk away for the day. Flip the meat once or twice if you can, but don't worry if you can't.

Just before you're ready to feast, stir in the reserved spices, brightening their flavors as you get ready for dinner. With the meat still in the slow cooker, tug and pull it into small shreds with a pair of tongs or forks. Stir the works together evenly.

You can make the coleslaw days in advance or just before you build the sandwiches. Simply whisk the honey, mustard, vinegar, olive oil, salt and hot sauce together in a large bowl until smooth, then add the coleslaw mix and thoroughly toss to evenly distribute the dressing flavors.

Build your sandwiches, and serve and share!

> ## FAMILY FLAVORS
> Every family cook should know how to divide food evenly. It's an essential survival skill and easy to master. Once you've stirred the shredded meat into the sauce, level the surface with your spoon. With the spoon, divide the works into two halves, then into four quarters. Each quadrant is easily divided into thirds, giving you 12 portions.

THESE SIMPLE SOFT TACOS ARE FILLED WITH THE STREET FOOD FLAVORS OF SUNNY Mexico. Your slow cooker is their ticket to your kitchen. Those big, flashy supermarket taco kits with their mysterious spice packages for ground beef are okay now and then, but they're also shortcuts. Here's how it's done on the street! MAKES ENOUGH FOR 16 TACOS OR SO

STREET TACOS

Preheat your slow cooker to its lowest setting.

Spoon the chili powder, cumin, oregano, salt, chipotle peppers, onions, garlic and tomatoes into the slow cooker and give everything a stir. Cut the beef into 4 even pieces and fit them into the slow cooker, flipping the works once or twice to evenly distribute the saucy flavors. Cover and walk away for the day. Flip the meat once or twice if you can, but don't worry if you can't.

When you're ready to open your taco bar, with the meat still in the slow cooker, tug and pull it into small shreds with a pair of tongs or forks. Splash in the lime zest and juice and stir the works together evenly.

Heap your tortillas with the delicious meaty filling, cheese and cabbage. Top with dollops of sour cream, splashes of hot sauce and a scattering of cilantro. Roll up or fold. Serve and share!

FOR THE MEAT

1 tablespoon (15 mL) of chili powder

1 tablespoon (15 mL) of ground cumin

1 tablespoon (15 mL) of dried oregano

1 teaspoon (5 mL) of sea salt

2 chipotle peppers in adobo sauce, minced

2 nice big onions, chopped

Cloves from 1 head of garlic, thinly sliced

A 28-ounce (796 mL) can of crushed, puréed or diced tomatoes

3 pounds (1.35 kg) or so of beef for roasting or stewing (such as blade, chuck or eye of round)

The zest and juice of 2 limes

FOR CRAFTING THE TACOS

16 small soft flour or corn tortillas

A heaping cup or two (275 to 500 mL) of shredded Cheddar, spicy Jack or taco-blend cheese

2 cups (500 mL) or so of finely shredded green cabbage (or iceberg lettuce in a pinch)

A cup (250 mL) or so of sour cream

Your favorite hot sauce

A few handfuls of fresh cilantro leaves and tender stems

FAMILY FLAVORS

Tacos are always a hit with the self-assembly crowd—especially kids. For fun and flavor, set up a taco station, then invite everyone to stuff their own tacos.

For an extra-special snappy crunch, slip a hard taco into the works. Gently fold a small soft tortilla around a standard-issue crisp tortilla before filling the works with flavor. As you eat, you'll snap the hard taco, but since its drippy contents are contained by the soft taco, that won't matter!

A SLOW COOKER FILLED WITH SIMPLE, COMFORTING INGREDIENTS IS A DELICIOUS thing to return home to after a long day. This dish is even better served with a pot of brown rice.

SERVES 4 TO 6

ROSEMARY APPLE BRAISED CHICKEN

1 chicken, cut into 10 pieces (2 wings,
  2 drumsticks, 2 thighs, 4 half-breasts)
  or 3 pounds (1.35 kg) or so of breasts,
  legs, drumsticks, thighs, even wings
2 large onions, chopped
6 to 8 garlic cloves, halved
4 firm local apples, each cored and
  cut into 8 wedges
4 sprigs of fresh rosemary
1 cup (250 mL) of apple cider or
  apple juice
1 cup (250 mL) of white wine
2 tablespoons (30 mL) of cider vinegar
2 teaspoons (10 mL) of salt
Lots of freshly ground pepper
1 bay leaf

Toss all the ingredients into your slow cooker. Stir the works a bit to evenly distribute all the flavors. Cover and cook on the lowest setting. Come back in 6 or 8 hours, cook some brown rice, serve and share!

FAMILY FLAVORS

You know how sometimes a dish comes with a super-fancy name so you figure it'll taste super-fancy and it must be really hard to make and it doesn't and it is? Not this time. Embellish your presentation any way you like, confident that your flavors are backing you up. It takes mere minutes to fill your slow cooker, but everyone will think you spent hours in the kitchen. Chardonnay, anyone?

AFTER CHASING A FEW COLORFUL CHICKENS AROUND THE HILLS OF NORTHERN Thailand, the local cooks and I made a dish like this. No one had a recipe, so I'm glad I took notes. They weren't worried about authenticity, and neither am I. They were just making dinner with what they had. A good strategy in any kitchen! SERVES 6 TO 8

CHIANG MAI CHICKEN WITH CURRIED COCONUT TOMATO BROTH

Preheat your slow cooker to its lowest setting.

Nestle the chicken, sweet potatoes and onions into the vessel. Add the tomatoes. Pour in half the can of coconut milk. Stir the ginger and curry paste into the remaining coconut milk, then add it to the works. Slip in the lime leaves. Cover and walk away for 6 or 8 hours.

With a slotted spoon, scoop the meat and vegetables into festive bowls. Stir the fish sauce into the broth. Ladle off and discard any extra oil if you like or realize that it's all flavor and richness and stir it back in before ladling the broth into the bowls. Top every bowl with carrots, bean sprouts and cilantro. Serve and share with limes for squeezing and seasoning.

FAMILY FLAVORS

I'll never forget sitting at a worn wooden table enjoying this dish with my new cook-friend's family. We laughed and pretended to understand each other as next week's chicken dinner ran around our feet. It reminded me of my home table and how important the simple act of sharing flavors and time with your family is.

FOR THE SLOW-COOKED CHICKEN

1 whole chicken, cut into 10 pieces
  (2 wings, 2 drumsticks, 2 thighs,
  4 half-breasts) or 3 pounds (1.35 kg)
  or so of breasts, legs, drumsticks,
  thighs, even wings

1 large sweet potato, peeled and cut
  into large chunks

1 large onion, peeled and cut into
  8 wedges

A 28-ounce (796 mL) can of
  diced tomatoes

A 19-ounce (540 mL) can of
  coconut milk

2 inches (5 cm) or so of frozen
  ginger, grated (2 heaping
  tablespoons/35 mL)

2 heaping tablespoons (35 mL) of mild
  yellow Thai curry paste (if you prefer
  more fragrant spicy heat, use green or
  red curry paste)

4 lime leaves (or the zest of 4 limes)

2 tablespoons (30 mL) of fish sauce

FOR TOPPING THE BOWLS

1 large carrot, peeled into strips with
  a vegetable peeler

A handful of bean sprouts

1 bunch of fresh cilantro

4 limes, halved

WHEN I WAS A KID, MY MOM USED TO MAKE "CHICKEN CATCH A TORY" ALL THE TIME. My brothers and I had no idea what the name meant (I'm not sure my mom did either). We knew what was in our bowls, though. Not stew—something else. We didn't know. It didn't matter, because what we did know was that we loved it. And seconds! SERVES 4 TO 6 WITH LOTS OF PASTA

OLD WORLD CHICKEN CACCIATORE

1 whole chicken, cut into 10 pieces
   (2 wings, 2 drumsticks, 2 thighs,
   4 half-breasts) or 3 pounds (1.35 kg)
   or so of breasts, legs, drumsticks,
   thighs, even wings
1 or 2 large onions, sliced
1 or 2 carrots, diced
Cloves from 1 head of garlic, halved
2 red bell peppers, diced
Leaves from 4 sprigs of fresh rosemary
A 28-ounce (796 mL) can of
   diced tomatoes
A 5.5-ounce (156 mL) can
   of tomato paste
1 cup (250 mL) of your favorite red
   or white wine
2 tablespoons (30 mL) of capers
1 tablespoon (15 mL) of red
   wine vinegar
1 teaspoon (5 mL) of salt
Lots of freshly ground pepper
1 pound (450 g) of egg noodles or your
   favorite pasta

Preheat your slow cooker to its lowest setting.

Fit the chicken pieces into the vessel. Add everything else except the noodles. Use your hands to mix all the flavors together as evenly as you can. Cover and walk away for the day.

Return. Set the table. Boil water. Cook the egg noodles. Serve and share! It's that simple. And that delicious!

FAMILY FLAVORS

Forty years ago my brothers and I loved my mom's version of the Mediterranean diet, long before it was trendy. And today it tastes even better! You can skip the normal messy step of browning the chicken and vegetables in oil first. The long braise yields much the same flavor.

CRAVING BARBECUED RIBS? IN A HURRY AND FEELING PRESSURED? TRY CHANNELING that pressure into some beefy ribs with some beefy technology. Your pressure cooker will have you feeling better in no time. Throw in some potatoes and classic BBQ flavor—one pot, one meal. If you don't have a pressure cooker yet, go get one. Don't be intimidated. Half the world uses these things. SERVES 4 OR, GRUDGINGLY, 6

FAST RIBS

Splash, pour, measure and sprinkle the water, barbecue sauce, mustard, molasses, vinegar, cumin, chili powder, salt and garlic into your pressure cooker. Stir together, evenly mixing the flavors. Fit the ribs and potatoes into the works. Bring to a furious boil, then reduce the heat to a slow, steady simmer. Fit the lid onto the pot and cook for 20 minutes. Turn off the heat and, without opening, let rest for 10 minutes.

Carefully release any lingering pressure, unseal and reveal the works. Pour the steamy sauce into a bowl, leaving the meat and potatoes in the pot. Let the liquid rest for a few minutes, giving the fat a chance to float to the top. Carefully pour off at least half the fat, even most. Stir your fresh herb into the sauce. Fish the rib bones out of the pot. Reunite the meat, potatoes and sauce in the pot.

Enjoy the delicious ribs and potatoes as is or feel free to stir in further finishing flavors and flourishes of your choice. Serve and share!

1 cup (250 mL) of water

1 cup (250 mL) of your favorite
   barbecue sauce

¼ cup (60 mL) of yellow mustard

¼ cup (60 mL) of molasses

2 tablespoons (30 mL) of red, white
   or cider vinegar

1 tablespoon (15 mL) of ground cumin

1 tablespoon (15 mL) of chili powder

1 teaspoon (60 mL) of salt

6 to 8 garlic cloves, halved

4 pounds (1.8 kg) or so of beef short
   ribs, cut into manageable chunks

2 large potatoes (or 3 or 4 smaller),
   cut into large chunks

A handful or two of your favorite fresh
   green herb, coarsely chopped

FAMILY FLAVORS

Using a pressure cooker to infuse beef ribs with traditional flavors is a bit unconventional but it works spectacularly. Besides, when you're the family cook, your number one goal is to get healthy flavor on the table in a hurry. There's no time for authenticity arguments. The end justifies the means!

FAMILY MEALS
IN MINUTES

FAMILY RECIPES

WHEN MY DAD COOKED STEAK, HE PREFERRED A CAST-IRON SKILLET ON THE STOVE. His dad did it that way, and we didn't have a barbecue. My brothers and I just loved watching him cook those steaks, and these wonderful flavors were all part of the ritual. SERVES 5 OR 6

DAD'S STEAK WITH MUSTARD RUB AND SKILLET ONIONS

A 20-ounce (565 g) or so sirloin steak, or 2 strip loins (12 ounces/340 g each), or even flank steak
1 tablespoon (15 mL) of dry mustard
Kosher salt
Lots of freshly ground pepper
¼ cup (60 mL) of butter
3 or 4 onions, thinly sliced

FAMILY FLAVORS

When I was a kid, none of my friends' dads ever cooked in the kitchen, and my dad didn't very often either. Everybody's dad grilled outside in the summer, but none dared enter mom's kitchen. It was always a special occasion when my dad cooked a steak.

Steak needs sizzle, so turn on your fan, open the windows, wave your arms, consider covering your smoke detector with a shower cap. That sort of thing. Heat a large cast-iron skillet or your favorite heavy skillet over medium-high heat.

Lay the steak on a plate and heavily sprinkle both sides with the dry mustard, salt and pepper. Evenly rub the seasoning into the meat.

Add the butter to the hot pan, swirling until it's evenly sizzling and lightly browning. Add the steaks before the butter burns. Sear them on each side until they're deliciously browned and crusty, 5 minutes or so per side. Listen to the heat. A simmering pan means nothing. Sizzle is the sound of flavor. Too loud, though, and a sizzling pan quickly becomes a smoking-burning pan.

Rinse off the seasoning plate and rest the steak on it. Cover loosely with foil. Keep the heat going in the pan and toss in the onions. Stir and sauté as the onions soften and color. When the onions are lightly browned and aromatic, turn off the heat.

Place the rested steaks on a cutting board. Pour any accumulated juices on the plate into the onions. Thinly slice the steak and evenly divide the proceeds onto the waiting plates. Top the steak with the sizzling onions and serve with a flourish!

A WELL-MADE BURGER IS A PERFECT TARGET FOR A BLAST OF CREATIVE FLAVOR. This Tex-Mex twist, with the spicy salsa flavors and classic crunch of nachos, is always a crowd-pleaser.

MAKES 6 LARGE OR 8 SMALLER BURGERS

NACHO BURGERS

Build a hardwood fire and ultimately a bed of glowing coals. Or prepare and preheat your grill or stovetop griddle to high.

To make the burgers, have a clean plate on the counter and a few sheets of wax paper or plastic wrap nearby. Place the ground beef in a large bowl. Break it up a bit and spread it out evenly. Sprinkle the meat as evenly as you can with the cumin, oregano, salt, pepper and onions. Using your hands, thoroughly and evenly mix the works together. Form the proceeds into 6 or 8 evenly shaped thin burgers and place them on the plate, with the wax paper in between layers.

To ready the buns for the grill, stir the chili powder into the melted butter and brush the fragrant fat onto the cut sides of the buns. Just before grilling the burgers, toast the buns until lightly browned and delicious.

Grill the burgers until browned, 4 or 5 minutes a side. Move the finished burgers straight from the grill to their toasted buns so their juices soak into the bread. Top with the salsa, cheese, tortilla chips and bun tops. Serve and share!

FAMILY FLAVORS

It's always a good idea to be extra careful with ground beef of unknown origin. The processors did their best and so should you. Frequent hand washing and good kitchen cleanliness are part of being a good cook.

FOR THE BURGERS

2 pounds (900 g) of ground beef

2 tablespoons (30 mL) of ground cumin

2 tablespoons (30 mL) of dried oregano

1 teaspoon (5 mL) of salt

Lots of freshly ground pepper

1 onion, minced

FOR THE BURGER BUNS

1 teaspoon (5 mL) of chili powder

2 tablespoons (30 mL) of butter, melted

6 or 8 of your favorite burger buns

TO GARNISH THE BURGERS

1 heaping tablespoon (20 mL) of your favorite salsa per burger

¼ cup (60 mL) of any shredded cheese per burger

3 or 4 tortilla chips, crushed, per burger

HERE'S HOW TO STRETCH ONE BIG STEAK INTO DINNER FOR FOUR. GRILL IT, THEN thinly slice and toss it into golden roasted potatoes and vegetables. Hash! Traditionally made with leftover steak, but easily crafted fresh off the grill too. *SERVES 4 AS A MAIN COURSE OR 6 TO 8 AS A SIDE DISH*

STEAK HASH

2 zucchini, cut into 1-inch (2.5 cm) cubes

2 or 3 large baking potatoes, cut into 1-inch (2.5 cm) cubes

1 red bell pepper, cut into 1-inch (2.5 cm) cubes

2 large onions, cut into 1-inch (2.5 cm) cubes

2 tablespoons (30 mL) of vegetable oil or bacon fat

1 teaspoon (5 mL) of dried rosemary

1 teaspoon (5 mL) of salt

Lots of freshly ground pepper

A great big 12- to 14-ounce (340 to 400 g) strip loin, rib-eye or your favorite steak

1 bag (6 ounces/170 g) of baby spinach (about 8 cups/2 L)

2 green onions, thinly sliced

Preheat your oven to 425°F (220°C). Turn on your convection fan if you have one.

Toss the vegetables together with the oil, rosemary, salt and pepper. Scrape the vegetables into a baking pan or casserole dish and roast, stirring once or twice, until they are soft, 45 minutes or so.

While the veggies roast, grill the steak however you care to, to the doneness you prefer. Let it rest for about 10 minutes, then thinly slice.

Top the roasted vegetables with the steak and the baby spinach. Stir to combine the flavors and wilt the delicate leaves. Sprinkle with the green onions as you serve and share!

FAMILY FLAVORS

If you somehow have a leftover cooked or uncooked steak, this is a good dish to use it in. Skip the searing step. Simply slice the steak as thinly as possible. Stack several slices at a time and slice further into small, thin meaty bits. Toss them into the vegetables before you roast the works, and dinner will emerge complete from the oven.

FEW THINGS IN LIFE ARE MORE USEFUL THAN A SIMPLE, SPEEDY PASTA DISH. YOU CAN craft this one in the time it takes for water to boil and pasta to cook. Now that's an essential life skill!

SERVES 6 TO 8

SPEEDY ROTISSERIE CHICKEN PASTA

Bring a large pot of water to a furious boil. Season with lots of salt until the water tastes as pleasantly briny as a day at the beach. Toss in the pasta and cook until it is tender but chewy, 10 minutes or so.

Meanwhile, shred the chicken from its carcass, pulling and tugging as much meat from the bones as possible. Reserve the meat. Keep the bones to make a broth or discard them.

Scoop out ½ cup (125 mL) or so of the pasta water, then drain the pasta. Working quickly, return the steaming-hot pasta and the reserved cooking water to the pot over high heat. Stir in the Boursin cheese and the mustard until the cheese melts and a creamy-smooth sauce emerges. Add the chicken and the spinach, stirring until the tender leaves wilt. Season with pepper. Serve, share and savor!

1 pound (450 g) of penne

A store-bought rotisserie chicken

1 wheel (5.2 ounces/150 g) of your favorite Boursin cheese, at room temperature

1 tablespoon (30 mL) of Dijon mustard

1 bag (10 ounces/280 g) of fresh spinach

Lots of freshly ground pepper

FAMILY FLAVORS

Of all the healthy kitchen tricks I know, perhaps the one I use the most is wilting baby spinach. A jolt of last-second dark green goodness can easily finish a myriad of dishes—stews, soups, pastas, basically anything moist.

BAKED CHICKEN WINGS ARE BOMBPROOF. THEY'RE SO EASY TO MAKE THAT I CAN'T help but experiment with them. This version is one of my family's favorites. It's inspired by the mythical general who somehow lent his name to the popular fried dish on Chinese restaurant menus all over North America. MAKES 24 FULL WINGS

GENERAL TSO'S CHICKEN WINGS

FOR THE BAKED WINGS

1 cup (250 mL) of all-purpose flour

2 teaspoons (10 mL) of baking powder

2 teaspoons (10 mL) of sea salt

Lots of freshly ground pepper

4 eggs

24 whole chicken wings or 48 assorted flats and drums

½ cup (125 mL) of cornstarch

FOR THE FINISHING SAUCY TOUCHES

½ cup (125 mL) of white sugar

½ cup (125 mL) of ketchup

½ cup (125 mL) of water

¼ cup (60 mL) of white vinegar

2 tablespoons (30 mL) of toasted sesame oil

1 teaspoon (5 mL) of your favorite hot sauce

2 inches (5 cm) or so of frozen ginger, grated (about 2 tablespoons/30 mL)

2 tablespoons (30 mL) of soy sauce

2 tablespoons (30 mL) of cornstarch

¼ cup (60 mL) of sesame seeds

4 green onions, thinly sliced

Preheat your oven to 350°F (180°C). Turn on your convection fan if you have one. Line a large baking sheet with parchment paper or a nonstick baking mat.

Get the wings going. In a small bowl, whisk together the flour, baking powder, salt and pepper. Thoroughly whisk in the eggs. Tumble the wings into a large bowl and sprinkle evenly with the cornstarch. Toss evenly, coating every surface, nook and cranny with the powder. Pour the egg mixture over the wings and gently toss with your fingers, evenly coating the works. Neatly array skin side up on the baking sheet. Bake until the wings are tender, lightly browned and crisp, 1 hour or so.

Meanwhile, build the glazing sauce. Into a small saucepan, measure the sugar, ketchup, water, vinegar, sesame oil, hot sauce and ginger. Heat gently. In a small cup of some kind, stir together the soy sauce and cornstarch until dissolved. Pour the slurry into the simmering sauce, stirring gently as it thickens into a shiny sauce. Remove from the heat.

When the wings are done, transfer them to a large bowl and pour the sauce over them. Toss lightly once or twice, add the sesame seeds, and toss until the wings are evenly coated. Plate the proceeds and sprinkle with the green onions. Serve and share!

FAMILY FLAVORS

A trip to a Chinese restaurant is one of our family's favorite restaurant voyages, but the classic General Tso flavors are always found on tender boneless chicken chunks, not chicken wings. (Maybe they're hidden among the authentic stuff on the back page, written in Mandarin.) Finally I just invented my own. They passed with flying colors the first time the kids got a taste of them!

THIS CLASSIC TWO-STEP METHOD FOR A PAN OF PORK CHOPS WORKS EVERY TIME. Sear first, then cover the works and lower the heat, thereby forming a quick finishing oven. Too easy! And too tasty with this tangy orange mustard sauce. SERVES 4

A PAN OF PORK CHOPS WITH MARMALADE MUSTARD PAN SAUCE

Heat your favorite large, heavy skillet over medium-high heat. Pat the chops dry with paper towels and place them on a plate. Sprinkle with the salt and pepper, turning the meat with tongs a few times to evenly coat the works. Pour the oil into the center of the hot pan. Spoon the butter into the puddle (the oil prevents the butter from burning). Swirl and sizzle until the delicate butter is lightly browned. Fill the pan with the pork chops and sear the meat until browned and crusted on the bottom, about 5 minutes. Flip, cover tightly and reduce the heat to the lowest setting. Cook for 3 or 4 minutes more.

Remove the chops to a plate and loosely cover with foil while you quickly craft their sauce. Return the heat to medium-high, splash in the orange juice and stir in the marmalade, mustard, tarragon and Worcestershire sauce. Bring to a furious boil and continue cooking, stirring now and then, until the sauce is thick and smooth, about 5 minutes. Spoon the sauce over the chops, serve and share!

FOR THE CHOPS

4 thick-cut pork chops, each about
 1 inch (2.5 cm) thick
1 teaspoon (1 mL) of salt
Lots of freshly ground pepper
1 tablespoon (15 mL) of vegetable oil
2 tablespoons (30 mL) of butter

FOR THE SAUCE

½ cup (125 mL) of orange juice
¼ cup (60 mL) of marmalade
2 tablespoons (30 mL) of grainy
 or Dijon mustard
1 teaspoon (5 mL) of dried tarragon
 or thyme
1 teaspoon (5 mL) of Worcestershire
 sauce

FAMILY FLAVORS

Every family needs a butcher. Get to know the one at your grocery store, or better yet, find a local specialty butcher. They're good folks to know. You can ask yours to cut you a brace of extra-thick chops or recommend other premium finds in their shop.

BORED WITH BEEF? TAKE ANOTHER BURGER PATH. THESE PATTIES ARE HUGE AND thin raw but contract to normal juicy size on the grill. They're fiery on the BBQ, so have a spray bottle of water ready for flare-ups. Easy to prepare and delicious in every way! MAKES 4 THICK JUICY BURGERS OR 6 SMALLER ONES

SPICED SAUSAGE BURGERS WITH ARUGULA AND HONEY MUSTARD RELISH

FOR THE PATTIES

2 pounds (900 g) of Italian sausage

4 garlic cloves

1 tablespoon (15 mL) of fennel seeds

1 tablespoon (15 mL) of cumin seeds

1 tablespoon (15 mL) of coriander seeds

FOR THE PICKLE RELISH

2 large dill pickles, minced

1 tablespoon (15 mL) of mayonnaise

1 tablespoon (15 mL) of sweet green pickle relish

1 tablespoon (15 mL) of honey

1 tablespoon (15 mL) of yellow mustard

TO BUILD THE BURGERS

4 thick slices of red onion, drizzled with oil

4 ciabatta buns, sliced in half

A 4-ounce (115 g) block of Parmigiano-Reggiano cheese

4 handfuls of arugula

Prepare and preheat your grill to its highest heat. Cut 5 large squares of wax or parchment paper.

To make the patties, slice through the casing of each sausage, from one end to the other, and release the meat into a large bowl. Grate the garlic onto the meat, using a microplane grater, cheese grater or the smallest holes of a box grater. Sprinkle in the fennel, cumin and coriander seeds. Using your hands, quickly and evenly blend the works together. Divide into 4 even portions. Roll each into a ball and place on a square of wax paper. Cover with another square of wax paper, then flatten into a thin patty 4 to 5 inches (10 to 12 cm) wide. Repeat with the other 3 burgers, reusing the top square of wax paper along the way, forming a stack of 4 patties and 5 papers ready to transport to the grill (or the refrigerator if you're wisely working in advance).

For the relish, in a small bowl, stir together the pickles, mayonnaise, relish, honey and mustard. Spread the zesty relish on the top half of the buns.

Using the wax paper squares, flip the patties onto the searing-hot grill. Fit in the red onion slices wherever you can; you may have to wait for the meat to shrink a bit. Grill the works until nicely seared on the bottom, 3 or 4 minutes. Carefully flip and finish cooking, 2 or 3 minutes more.

Move the burgers from the grill to the bun bottoms. Using a vegetable peeler, peel a few large shards of the cheese onto each burger. Top with the arugula, the grilled onions and the bun top. Serve and share!

FAMILY FLAVORS

Having a grill in your repertoire is always a good thing. Try to safely involve your kids in its rituals. The job of cleaning and maintaining our Big Green Egg often falls to my son Gabe, and it's a big help for Dad as we get ready to cook.

You CAN BANG OUT A BATCH OF FRIED RICE IN THE TIME IT TAKES FOR DELIVERY TO arrive. It's an easy formula. Your favorite stir-fry pan. A pile of shrimp. A few eggs and some other stuff. It all adds up to one delicious meal that always tastes better than take-out. The secret is to use leftover rice, so make a pot the night before. But if that doesn't work out, cook the rice the same night. The results will still be delicious—just a little softer. SERVES 4—NO LEFTOVERS, THOUGH

SPECIAL SHRIMP FRIED RICE

The secret to fried rice is leftover rice, so the day before, measure the rice, water, soy sauce and ginger into a saucepan and stir, bringing the works to a slow, steady simmer over medium-high heat. Cover tightly, set to the lowest possible heat, and cook for 20 minutes. Turn off the heat but don't touch the lid, and let rest for 10 minutes. Fluff with a fork and chill overnight.

Get out your wok or your biggest, heaviest nonstick skillet. Have a side plate and a couple of bowls on the side to temporarily hold things.

For the shrimp: Toss the shrimp into the hot pan, pour in the water and cover tightly. Bring to a furious boil, then reduce the heat and steam the shrimp until they just turn pink and are still tender, 5 minutes. Transfer to a bowl and set aside. Peel them when you get a chance.

For the eggs: Wipe out the pan and heat over medium-high heat while you whisk together the eggs and green onions. Splash the sesame oil into the pan, swirling it into a flavorful film. Slide in the egg. Swirl the works, forming an even, sizzling layer of quickly setting eggy goodness. Brown the bottom a bit, just a minute or two, then deftly flip and lightly brown the second side, 2 to 3 minutes in total. Slide the egg onto the side plate.

For the vegetables: Splash some vegetable oil into the pan. Spoon in the garlic and ginger, sautéing briefly to brighten their flavors. Toss in the red pepper and bean sprouts and sauté, sizzling and shaking for 3 or 4 minutes. Pour into a bowl.

It's time to fry some rice at last! Wipe out the pan and heat over the highest heat. Splash a pool of oil into the pan, swirling to coat the bottom with a thin film. Immediately add the rice and edamame, breaking up any clumps of rice, stirring constantly, sizzling and searing for 10 minutes or so. Add the soy sauce and oyster sauce. Stir in the peeled shrimp, the vegetables and the egg, breaking up the egg as you do so. Stir until heated through, another minute or so. Serve and share topped with scattered cashews and chow mein noodles.

FOR THE LEFTOVER RICE
2 cups (500 mL) of jasmine or other long-grain white rice
4 cups (2 L) of water
1 tablespoon (15 mL) of soy sauce
1 inch (2.5 cm) of frozen ginger, grated (or 1 tablespoon/15 mL dried)

FOR THE STEAMED SHRIMP
1 pound (450 g) of any-sized frozen shrimp, unpeeled, thawed
¼ cup (60 mL) of water

FOR THE FRIED EGGS
4 eggs
2 green onions, thinly sliced
1 teaspoon (5 mL) of toasted sesame oil

FOR THE SEARED VEGETABLES
1 teaspoon (5 mL) of vegetable oil, preferably grapeseed
8 garlic cloves, minced
1 inch (2.5 cm) or so of fresh ginger, peeled and thinly sliced
1 red bell pepper, cut into thin strips
A handful of bean sprouts

FOR THE FRIED RICE
1 teaspoon (5 mL) of vegetable oil, preferably grapeseed
4 cups (1 L) of leftover rice
1 cup (250 mL) of frozen shelled edamame or green peas
¼ cup (60 mL) of soy sauce
2 tablespoons (30 mL) of oyster sauce or fish sauce

FOR THE FINISHING FLOURISHES
1 cup (250 mL) of cashews
1 cup (250 mL) of crispy chow mein noodles

FAMILY FLAVORS
- - - - - - - - - -
The woks at your local Chinese restaurant get a blast of heat hotter than any other stove in any other restaurant, let alone your kitchen. So the ingredients don't overwhelm your heat at home, each of the parts are cooked separately. The big payoff comes at the end, when all those flavors combine with the rice.

THIS IS A DELICIOUS WAY TO TRANSFORM A FEW ORDINARY PIECES OF FRESH SALMON into a spicy and crispy baked revelation, to be savored with lots of big, bright salad-like salsa flavors.

SERVES 4 TO 6

CHILI CORNMEAL CRUSTED SALMON WITH AVOCADO SALSA

FOR THE SALSA

2 avocados, scooped and diced

2 green onions, sliced

1 pint (500 mL) of cherry tomatoes, halved

A big handful of chopped fresh cilantro, a few sprigs reserved for garnish

The zest and juice of 2 limes

½ teaspoon (2 mL) of salt

½ teaspoon (2 mL) of your favorite hot sauce

¼ teaspoon (1 mL) of toasted sesame oil

FOR THE CRISPY CRUSTY SALMON

¼ cup (60 mL) of fine yellow cornmeal

2 tablespoons (30 mL) of chili powder

2 tablespoons (30 mL) of brown sugar

1 teaspoon (5 mL) of salt

4 to 6 fresh skinless salmon fillets (5 to 6 ounces/140 to 170 g each)

Preheat your oven to 425°F (220°C). Line a baking sheet with parchment paper and lightly oil the paper.

Make the salsa first. In a medium bowl, combine all the salsa ingredients. Toss and stir, evenly distributing the bright flavors. Set aside.

Move on to the salmon. In a shallow bowl, whisk together the cornmeal, chili powder, brown sugar and salt. Dredge the salmon through the crunchy coating, evenly and thoroughly coating each piece, shaking the excess back into the dish for the next piece. Position on the baking sheet and roast until cooked through, tender and juicy, 10 minutes or so.

Scoop a generous mound of the salsa onto each plate. Top with a piece of crispy crusty salmon and a festive sprig of cilantro. Serve and share!

FAMILY FLAVORS

Anything you can do to get your family eating fish is a good thing. Salmon may be good for you and delicious, but sometimes to get it out the door it helps to gussy it up with a bright blast of sunny southwestern flavor.

THE RICH GOODNESS OF SALMON ANCHORS THE SHARP, SNAPPY FLAVORS OF THIS snack-inspired crust. A ladleful of tender, fragrant edamame stew brings even more Asian flavor to your bowl. SERVES 4 TO 6

WASABI PEA CRUSTED SALMON WITH GINGER EDAMAME STEW

Preheat your oven to 425°F (220°C). Line a baking sheet with parchment paper and lightly oil the paper.

For the salmon, toss the wasabi peas into a resealable bag and give them a good crushing with the bottom of a heavy skillet or bowl. Measure in the oil and massage the works into a paste. Cluster the salmon fillets directly next to each other on the baking sheet. Top the fish with a thick, even coating of the crushed-pea paste. Use a knife to separate the fillets from each other for faster, even cooking. Bake until cooked through and tender, 15 minutes or so.

Meanwhile, cook the edamame. Spoon the butter into a medium saucepan over medium-high heat and swirl until sizzling. Add the garlic and ginger and continue sizzling and stirring for 2 or 3 minutes. Splash in the soy sauce and water, then pour in the edamame. Stir briefly. Cover tightly and steam until the edamame are tender, 5 minutes or so. Stir in the bean sprouts for the last minute or so of cooking.

Serve and share the crispy salmon with the brightly flavored edamame.

FOR THE CRUSTED SALMON

1 cup (250 mL) of wasabi peas

1 tablespoon (15 mL) of toasted sesame oil

4 to 6 fresh skinless salmon fillets (5 to 6 ounces/140 to 170 g each)

FOR THE GINGER EDAMAME STEW

1 tablespoon (15 mL) of butter

2 or 3 garlic cloves, grated

1 inch (2.5 cm) of frozen ginger, grated

1 tablespoon (15 mL) of soy sauce

1 tablespoon (15 mL) of water

A 1-pound (450 g) bag of frozen shelled edamame

A big handful of tender bean sprouts

FAMILY FLAVORS

We love the snappy fun of wasabi peas in a quick snack blend. They're an easy way to spark interest in a salmon feed and perform admirably as the base for this ingenious crust. The oven's heat tones down their spicy heat a bit.

MEATLESS MONDAYS

FAMILY RECIPES

THE PERFECT VEGGIE BURGER BLENDS THE GRAINS AND LEGUMES WITH LOTS OF savory flavors. That's pretty easy. The challenge is to ensure moistness and strength. The patties have to stay together on the grill. Chia seeds are the magic ingredient here. They absorb moisture while providing binding strength and structure. MAKES 8 THICK BURGERS

CHIA VEGGIE BURGER

FOR THE MUSHROOM LENTIL BASE

2 tablespoons (30 mL) of vegetable oil

1 onion, finely chopped

4 garlic cloves, sliced

1 pound (450 g) of any fresh
 mushrooms, sliced

1 cup (250 mL) of brown rice

1 cup (250 mL) of green lentils

3 cups (750 mL) of water

2 tablespoons (30 mL) of dried thyme,
 tarragon or oregano

1 bay leaf

FOR THE BURGER BLEND

1 cup (250 mL) of chia seeds

½ cup (125 mL) of peanut or
 almond butter

2 tablespoons (30 mL) of miso paste

2 tablespoons (30 mL) of soy sauce

1 sweet potato, peeled and grated

FOR THE BURGER WORKS

4 whole-grain burger buns, split
 and toasted

A few squeezes of ceremonial ketchup

4 handfuls of Bibb or leaf lettuce

Thinly sliced tomatoes

Thinly sliced red onions

Thinly sliced dill pickles

For the lentil base, splash the oil into a large, heavy skillet over medium-high heat, swirling into a thin film. Toss in the onions and garlic and sauté as the onions soften, 2 or 3 minutes. Stir in the mushrooms. Cover and continue cooking, stirring now and then, until the mushrooms have released their savory moisture, about 10 minutes. Measure in the rice and lentils. Pour in the water and add the thyme and bay leaf. Bring to a furious boil, then immediately reduce the heat to a slow, steady simmer. Cover tightly and cook until the rice and lentils are tender but still a bit chewy, 20 minutes. Remove from the heat and let rest for 10 minutes without removing the lid.

For the burger blend, spoon the mushroom flavor base into your food processor. Add the chia seeds, nut butter, miso paste and soy sauce. Pulse until thoroughly smooth, scraping down the sides once or twice. Transfer the works to a bowl and stir in the sweet potato by hand. Cover with plastic wrap and refrigerate, giving the chia seeds time to work their inherent magic, swelling and strengthening the protein-rich blend, about 20 minutes.

Line a baking sheet with parchment paper and lightly oil the paper. Shape the burger mixture into 8 thick patties and place them on the baking sheet. Prepare and preheat your grill, griddle or oven to 400°F (200°C) or more.

Grill or sauté the burgers until firm but tender, 8 minutes or so per side. Alternatively, bake for 20 minutes, flipping once. Build a magnificent burger with the buns and garnishes. Serve and share!

FAMILY FLAVORS

You can put healthy meals on the table all you want, but if your kids don't like the look or texture of their meal, they're not going to eat it. This burger easily passes the test on its way straight to gobble.

THIS TRADITIONAL TAPAS BAR SNACK IS SOMETIMES SERVED BETWEEN TWO SLICES of rustic crusty bread. It's just as delicious served plain. Either way, the bright pickled tomatoes steal the show. This is the sort of dish you'll quickly come to crave. SERVES 4 TO 6, EVEN 8 WITH SMALLER BRUNCH SERVINGS

SPANISH OMELET WITH PICKLED CHERRY TOMATOES

Begin with the pickled tomatoes. Measure the onion, water, vinegar, sugar, coriander seeds, fennel seeds, mustard seeds and hot sauce into a medium saucepan. Bring to a slow, steady simmer. Continue simmering until the mixture is reduced by half, 10 minutes or so. Remove from the heat and stir in the tomatoes and green onions. Let rest for at least 10 minutes, even overnight.

For the omelet, heat a large nonstick sauté pan over medium-high heat. Swirl in the oil. Add the onions and garlic, briefly sautéing to soften the onions. Add the potatoes and sauté a few minutes more. Cover tightly and reduce the heat. Cook, sizzling slightly, shaking the works two or three times, until the potatoes are tender and lightly browned, 20 minutes or so.

Whisk the eggs with the oregano, salt and pepper. Gently stir in the feta cheese. Add the potato mixture to the bowl, stir to thoroughly coat the works and return to the sauté pan. Cover tightly and cook until firm but still tender, 5 or 6 minutes. Loosen the omelet from the pan with a rubber spatula. With a strong grip and a few folded kitchen towels or a potholder, invert the pan, releasing the omelet onto the lid (if it's flat) or a large plate. Carefully slide it back into the pan and cook for another few minutes, firming and lightly browning the bottom.

Slice into wedges in the pan using the rubber spatula. Serve and share with spoonfuls of the pickled tomatoes.

FAMILY FLAVORS

Eggs are an excellent choice for regular rotation in your dinner cycle. They're a strong protein source, economical, nutritious, easy and always delicious.

FOR THE PICKLED CHERRY TOMATOES

1 red onion, thinly sliced

¼ cup (60 mL) of water or tomato juice

¼ cup (60 mL) of cider vinegar

2 tablespoons (30 mL) of white sugar

1 tablespoon (15 mL) of coriander seeds

1 tablespoon (15 mL) of fennel seeds

1 teaspoon (5 mL) of mustard seeds

¼ teaspoon (1 mL) of your favorite hot sauce

1 pint (500 mL) of cherry tomatoes, halved

2 green onions, thinly sliced

FOR THE POTATO OMELET

½ cup (125 mL) of olive oil

1 large onion, sliced

8 garlic cloves, thinly sliced

4 baking potatoes, peeled and thinly sliced

6 to 8 eggs

1 teaspoon (5 mL) of dried oregano

½ teaspoon (2 mL) of salt

Lots of freshly ground pepper

4 ounces (115 g) of feta cheese, crumbled (1 cup/250 mL or so)

THIS SPECTACULAR LASAGNA IS EASY TO BUILD, WITH A SPICY BLACK BEAN BASE and tortillas in place of the traditional noodles. SERVES 4 TO 6, WITH LEFTOVERS

TORTILLA LASAGNA

1 tablespoon (15 mL) of vegetable oil

1 large onion, chopped

4 garlic cloves, sliced

2 tablespoons (30 mL) of brown sugar

1 tablespoon (15 mL) of chili powder

1 teaspoon (5 mL) of ground cumin

1 teaspoon (5 mL) of dried oregano

½ teaspoon (2 mL) of sea salt

A 19-ounce (540 mL) can of black beans, drained and rinsed

2 cups (500 mL) of frozen corn

2 cups (500 mL) of your favorite salsa

1 bag (12 ounces/340 g) of shredded taco-blend cheese or 12 ounces (340 g) shredded Cheddar cheese

10 small corn tortillas

Preheat your oven to 375°F (190°C).

Splash the oil into a large, heavy skillet over medium-high heat. Toss in the onions and garlic and sauté until the onions soften, just 2 or 3 minutes. Add the brown sugar, chili powder, cumin, oregano and salt. Stir and sizzle for a minute or two more. Stir in the beans, corn and salsa. Continue cooking until heated through. Remove from the heat.

Spoon half the bean mixture evenly into your lasagna pan. Sprinkle with one-third of the cheese. Cut 1 tortilla in quarters and fit firmly into the corners. Cut another 2 in half and complete the ends and sides of the layer. Overlap 2 whole tortillas in the middle. Press firmly into place. Make 1 more layer in the same manner, and sprinkle with the remaining cheese. Bake until heated through and the cheese is lightly browned, 30 minutes or so. Cool in the pan until the lasagna firms a bit, 10 minutes or so. Slice, scoop, serve and share!

FAMILY FLAVORS
- - - - - - - - - - - -
Make a batch of this lasagna on the weekend and refrigerate for the week ahead (or freeze it). Once cold, it's very firm and a cinch to portion for school or work lunchboxes.

B IG, BOLD, MYSTERIOUS MOROCCAN SPICES AND FLAVORS ARE SOME OF MY FAVORITE in the world. They add lots of character to this couscous stuffing along with dried legumes, grain, fruit and nuts—the flavors of arid desert cooking. MAKES 6 STUFFED PEPPERS

MOROCCAN STUFFED PEPPERS

Preheat your oven to 375°F (190°C). Find a baking dish large enough to snugly fit the bell peppers.

In a medium saucepan, measure the juice, marmalade, nut butter, ras el hanout, lemon zest and juice, hot sauce and salt. Thoroughly whisk, and then, while stirring, bring the works to a furious boil. Immediately reduce the heat to a slow, steady simmer. Stir in the chickpeas, carrot, raisins and nuts. Return to a simmer. Stir in the couscous, turn off the heat, cover and let rest as the grain softens and absorbs the moisture, at least 10 minutes.

Meanwhile, ready the bell peppers. Slice the top inch (2.5 cm) off each pepper. Carefully scoop out and discard the seeds and any white membranes from the inside of the peppers and the lids. Evenly spoon the couscous into the peppers. Arrange the peppers in the baking dish and top with their lids. Pour the water into the pan. Transfer to the oven and bake until the stuffing is hot, 60 minutes, or better 90 minutes for tasty browning. Quickly lift each lid, top the stuffing with a thick layer of sliced mint and replace the lid. Serve and share with a flourish!

1 cup (250 mL) of orange or
  tomato juice
¼ cup (60 mL) of marmalade
¼ cup (60 mL) of any nut butter
1 tablespoon (15 mL) of ras el hanout
  (or 1 teaspoon/5 mL each curry
  powder, cinnamon and ground cumin)
The zest and juice of 1 lemon
1 teaspoon (5 mL) of your favorite
  hot sauce
½ teaspoon (2 mL) of sea salt
A 19-ounce (540 mL) can of chickpeas,
  drained and rinsed
1 carrot, shredded
½ cup (125 mL) of raisins or sliced
  dried apricots
½ cup (125 mL) of pine nuts
  or pistachios
1 cup (250 mL) of couscous
6 red, yellow or orange bell peppers
2 cups (500 mL) of water
Leaves from 1 bunch of mint, very
  thinly sliced

FAMILY FLAVORS

This dish is such a showstopper that your family won't really notice the meatless issue unless you point it out to them.

A LADLEFUL OF BRIGHTLY FLAVORED RED LENTILS SERVED OVER AROMATIC WHITE rice is everyday Indian comfort food for hundreds of millions of people. Try a tasty bowl and you just might end up joining the flavor fun! SERVES 4 TO 6

RICE AND DAL

FOR THE DAL

1 tablespoon (15 mL) of butter

1 large onion, chopped

2 or 3 garlic cloves, minced

1 tablespoon (15 mL) of curry powder

1 cup (250 mL) of red lentils, rinsed

3 cups (750 mL) of water

½ teaspoon (2 mL) of sea salt

FOR THE RICE

1 tablespoon (15 mL) of butter

1 large onion, minced

2 or 3 garlic cloves, minced

1 cup (250 mL) of white basmati rice

2 cups (500 mL) of water

½ teaspoon (2 mL) of sea salt

Lots of freshly ground pepper

A handful of chopped fresh cilantro

Begin with the dal. Melt and sizzle the butter in a small saucepan over medium-high heat, then toss in the onions and garlic. Cook, stirring, lightly browning and softening the onions, just 3 or 4 minutes. Sprinkle in the curry powder and stir for a moment to brighten the flavor. Add the lentils and water. Bring to a furious boil, then reduce the heat to the slowest, steadiest simmer possible. Continue cooking until the lentils are tender and translucent, 30 minutes or so. Season with salt and stir the works until lightly mashed.

While the lentils simmer, make the rice. Melt and sizzle the butter in a small saucepan over medium-high heat. Add the onions and garlic and cook, just like before, until the onions are soft and lightly browned. Add the rice and stir for a few minutes to lightly toast the grains. Pour in the water and sprinkle in the salt and pepper. Bring to a furious boil, then reduce the heat to the slowest, steadiest simmer possible. Cover and cook until the rice is tender, 15 minutes or so. Let it rest with the lid on for 5 minutes or so as the grains finish absorbing the moisture. Serve and share the dal over the rice, topped with lots of chopped cilantro.

FAMILY FLAVORS

Every family has its go-to comfort foods. The flavors that remind them of meals past and times spent together. The bright, hearty flavors of rice and dal are some of our favorites. In our family, they're just as iconic as mashed potatoes.

TOFU IN THE OVEN ROASTING, A SMALL POT OF BROWN RICE COOKING, A PAN OF spicy peanut goodness simmering and a stir-fry pan sizzling away. This is the big leagues, keeping an eye on three pans *and* your oven. No worries, you'll be an all-star! This one's destined to become a family favorite, especially if you all cook it together. SERVES 2 AS A MAIN OR 4 AS A SIDE

BROCCOLI TOFU WITH SPICY PEANUT SAUCE AND BROWN RICE

Begin with the tofu. Preheat your oven to 400°F (200°C) and lightly oil a baking sheet or line with parchment paper. Toss the tofu with the vegetable oil and lay out in a single layer on the baking sheet. Bake until golden brown, about 30 minutes.

Meanwhile, measure the rice, water and miso into a small saucepan. Stir briefly and bring to a furious boil, then reduce the heat to the slowest, steadiest simmer possible. Cover tightly and cook until the rice is tender, 30 minutes. Turn off the heat but don't touch the lid, resting a further 10 minutes.

At the same time, make the sauce. Measure the ingredients into a small saucepan and heat through slowly, stirring until smooth and hot. Cover and turn off the heat. As soon as the tofu is done, stir it into the sauce to marinate a bit.

Ready the engines for the stir-fry. Heat your biggest, heaviest nonstick skillet over medium-high heat. Splash 1 teaspoon (5 mL) of the sesame oil into the pan and immediately toss in the onions, garlic and ginger. Swirl and sauté for a moment to release their flavors, then add the broccoli, water, soy sauce and remaining 1 teaspoon (5 mL) of sesame oil. Cover and steam until the broccoli is bright and tender, 2 or 3 minutes.

Combine the broccoli, tofu and rice in a big bowl or keep them separate for presentation. Serve and share, topping big bowls of rice with spicy tofu, bright broccoli, scattered peanuts, green onions and crunchy noodles.

FAMILY FLAVORS

This is a seriously tasty, healthy dish, but it can be memorable for another reason. Get your family to help. Everybody looks after a component. Many hands make light work, and you can gather, prepare and share the works together.

FOR THE BAKED TOFU

1 pound (450 g) of firm tofu, cut into 1-inch (2.5 cm) cubes

2 tablespoons (30 mL) of vegetable oil

FOR THE BROWN RICE

1 cup (250 mL) of brown rice

2 cups (500 mL) of water

1 tablespoon (15 mL) of miso paste or soy sauce

FOR THE SAUCE

1 cup (250 mL) of peanut butter

1 cup (250 mL) of water

¼ cup (60 mL) of soy sauce

¼ cup (60 mL) of molasses

2 tablespoons (30 mL) of cider vinegar

1 tablespoon (15 mL) of red pepper jelly

1 teaspoon (5 mL) of your favorite hot sauce

FOR THE STIR-FRY

2 teaspoons (10 mL) of toasted sesame oil

2 onions, thinly sliced

6 to 8 garlic cloves, minced

1 inch (2.5 cm) of frozen ginger, grated

1 bunch of broccoli

2 tablespoons (30 mL) of water

1 tablespoon (15 mL) of soy sauce

FOR GARNISH

½ cup (125 mL) of chopped peanuts

2 green onions, thinly sliced

A handful of crispy chow mein noodles

IT'S EASIER TO TRANSFORM A BALL OF FROZEN PIZZA DOUGH AND A CAN OF PIZZA sauce into a round of calzones than into pizza. Just add cheese, aromatic herbs and fresh cherry tomatoes for a hearty meal that's on the table almost faster than you can find that take-out pizza menu. MAKES 4 CALZONES

TRIPLE-CHEESE CALZONES

A 7-ounce (207 mL) can of pizza
  or tomato sauce
½ cup (125 mL) of ricotta cheese
2 cups (500 mL) of shredded
  mozzarella cheese
½ cup (125 mL) of freshly grated
  Parmigiano-Reggiano cheese
1 teaspoon (5 mL) of dried oregano
Leaves from 1 bunch of fresh basil
1 pint (500 mL) of cherry tomatoes,
  halved
1 pound (450 g) of fresh or thawed
  frozen pizza dough
A few splashes of olive oil

Preheat your oven to 400°F (200°C). Turn on your convection fan if you have one. Line a baking sheet with parchment paper.

In a medium bowl, whisk together the pizza sauce and ricotta cheese. Stir in the mozzarella, Parmesan, oregano, basil and tomatoes.

Divide the dough into 4 equal pieces and shape each piece into a ball. Lightly flour your work surface, your hands, a rolling pin and the dough balls. One at a time, flatten and roll out each dough ball into a 10-inch (25 cm) circle, rolling from the center, flipping and turning the dough, taking care not to flatten the edges.

Mound one-quarter of the filling onto each round just below the "equator." Fold the dough over the filling. Starting at one end, roll the edges tightly together, continuing around to the other end and sealing the filling inside the calzone. Fold any little dough tail under. Transfer to the baking sheet, lightly brush the tops with oil and cut 2 small vent holes in each for steam to escape. Bake until golden brown, about 30 minutes. Serve and share!

FAMILY FLAVORS
- - - - - - - - - - - - -
There are as many ways to fill a calzone as there are cooks to stuff it. This is an easy recipe to add your family's twists to. Chopped vegetables, bacon, breakfast sausage, sliced ham and spoonfuls of leftover taco filling have all found their way into our calzones.

THIS DISH IS PACKED WITH HEALTHY INGREDIENTS, BUT DON'T WORRY, NO ONE WILL notice, because they'll be so impressed with all the flavor in their bowl. Stews are easy to make too. It's hard to mess up tossing a bunch of flavors into a pot and cooking them until they're tender. It's even easier when you don't have to muck about with meat! SERVES 4 TO 6

SWEET POTATO CHICKPEA STEW

Splash the vegetable oil into a large pot over medium-high heat. Toss in the onions and garlic and cook, stirring, as the onions soften, 5 minutes or so. Sprinkle in the curry and stir for a few moments to brighten its flavor. Toss in the sweet potatoes, chickpeas, water and salt. Bring to a slow, steady simmer, then simmer long enough for the sweet potato to soften, 20 minutes or so.

Pour in the coconut milk, peas and tomatoes. Continue cooking just long enough to heat everything through. Season with the hot sauce and lime zest and juice. Serve and share with the cilantro sprinkled over every bowl.

2 tablespoons (30 mL) of vegetable oil
1 large onion, chopped
4 garlic cloves, sliced
2 tablespoons (30 mL) of curry powder
2 large sweet potatoes, peeled and cut into 1-inch (2.5 cm) cubes
A 19-ounce (540 mL) can of chickpeas, drained and rinsed
4 cups (1 L) of water
1 teaspoon (5 mL) of salt
A 14-ounce (400 mL) can of coconut milk
2 cups (500 mL) of fresh or frozen green peas
1 pint (500 mL) of cherry tomatoes, halved
½ teaspoon (2 mL) of your favorite hot sauce
The zest and juice of 1 lime
A handful of fresh cilantro sprigs

FAMILY FLAVORS

Life can be hectic, and the last place we need more hassle is in the kitchen. That's why I'm such a big fan of canned chickpeas. They're easy to open, easy to dress up and easy to enjoy. I can relax when there are a few cans ready in my pantry for quick and easy dishes like this one.

THIS IS AN EXCELLENT VEGETARIAN MAIN COURSE, BUT IT'S EQUALLY AT HOME AS A simple side dish for any meat too. It's spectacularly easy to make and equally spectacular to serve.

SERVES 4

BLACK BEAN CORNMEAL COBBLER

FOR THE FILLING

1 tablespoon (15 mL) of vegetable oil

1 large onion, chopped

4 garlic cloves, sliced

1 red bell pepper, chopped

1 teaspoon (5 mL) of ground cumin

A 28-ounce (796 mL) can of
  diced tomatoes

A 19-ounce (540 mL) can of black
  beans, drained and rinsed

FOR THE DUMPLINGS

1 cup (250 mL) of all-purpose flour

1 cup (250 mL) of yellow cornmeal

1 teaspoon (5 mL) of white sugar

1 teaspoon (5 mL) of salt

1 cup (250 mL) of milk

½ cup (125 mL) of butter, melted

2 cups (500 mL) of shredded Cheddar
  or taco-blend cheese

For the filling, splash the vegetable oil into a large sauté pan over medium-high heat. Toss in the onions and garlic and cook, stirring, as the onions soften, 5 minutes or so. Toss in the bell pepper and cumin. Sauté just long enough to heat through and brighten the flavors, a few minutes more. Stir in the tomatoes and black beans. Bring to a slow, steady simmer, then turn off the heat while you make the dumplings.

Measure the flour, cornmeal, sugar and salt into a large bowl. Whisk thoroughly. Pour in the milk and melted butter. Stir until thoroughly combined. Add the cheese and stir just long enough to evenly combine the works. Using a large soupspoon, drop the batter evenly over the stew. Return the works to a slow simmer and cook for 10 minutes or so. Cover tightly and continue cooking 10 more minutes. Serve and share!

FAMILY FLAVORS

You don't have to have a vegetarian in the house to include a regular repertoire of meatless dishes on your family's table. Most of the world's food revolves around ingredients other than meat, and yours can too. Anyway, dishes like this one are so tasty, no one's even likely to notice the missing meat!

EVERY JULY, MY COMMUNITY ON PRINCE EDWARD ISLAND HOSTS THE VILLAGE FEAST, a rollicking foodie extravaganza, steak dinner for a thousand and feel-good fundraiser. The event benefits our local food bank, and every year we raise enough money to build a school cookhouse in rural Kenya too. Githeri is the sort of simple, nourishing staple that's always on the table in Kenya, and we serve it at our Village Feast. SERVES 4

KENYAN GITHERI

Splash the oil into a medium saucepan over medium-high heat, then toss in the onions and garlic. Cook, stirring, until the onions are soft and lightly browned, just 3 or 4 minutes. Sprinkle in the curry powder and stir for a moment or two to brighten its flavor.

Pour in the tomatoes, corn and beans. Sprinkle in the salt and pepper. Bring to a furious boil, then reduce the heat to a slow, steady simmer. Stir in the kale and cook until it's tender and bright green, 10 minutes or so. Serve and share!

1 tablespoon (15 mL) of vegetable oil

1 large onion, chopped

3 garlic cloves, minced

1 tablespoon (15 mL) of curry powder

A 28-ounce (796 mL) can of diced or chopped tomatoes

4 cups (1 L) of fresh or frozen corn

A 14-ounce (398 mL) can of any cooked beans, drained and rinsed

½ teaspoon (2 mL) of salt

Lots of freshly ground pepper

A large bunch of kale, trimmed and chopped

FAMILY FLAVORS

Food is universal. Every time we enjoy this dish, I'm able to remind my family that this is how families in Kenya eat. It's a delicious reminder that food connects us all.

VEGETABLES & WHOLE GRAINS

FAMILY RECIPES

YOU HAVEN'T LIVED UNTIL YOU'VE ROASTED A TOMATO AND DISCOVERED THE magical flavor and texture within. It's there, locked inside every tomato just waiting for you to roast and release it. SERVES AS MANY AS YOU HAVE TOMATOES

HERB ROAST TOMATOES

Vine-ripened tomatoes

FOR EACH TOMATO

A sprig of fresh thyme
2 garlic cloves
1 teaspoon (5 mL) of your best olive oil
A sprinkle each of salt and freshly
    ground pepper
A splash or two of your very best
    balsamic vinegar

Preheat your oven to 400°F (200°C). Ready a festive baking dish or ovenproof sauté pan just large enough to snugly fit the tomatoes.

Using a sharp or serrated knife, cut an X into each tomato, through its stem end and down to just below the "equator." Lay a sprig of fresh thyme through the middle of each tomato one way, and stuff the garlic into the 2 remaining ends the other way. Drench the works with great olive oil and season lightly, keeping in mind the flavor concentration ahead. Cram the tomatoes together into the pan.

Roast for at least 60 minutes, but better to wait another 20. The tomatoes will be soft and caramelized and full of intense flavor. Drizzle with the balsamic vinegar. Transcendental! Serve and share!

FAMILY FLAVORS

Sometimes we overlook intense flavor hidden right under our noses. There's nothing elusive about a tomato, but it does take some coaxing to reveal the hidden flavors of patient roasting.

’M A LIFELONG SAILOR, AND DOWN AT THE BEACH WE SAY, "RIG BIG OR STAY HOME."
Back home in the kitchen, that means if you cook some greens, you might as well cook a lot of greens! Here's an easy way to get a whole lot of healthy, hearty green flavor together using the time-honored method of steaming, this time with lots of browned butter to elevate the works. SERVES 4 TO 6, WITH LEFTOVERS, OR A PARTY OF 8 OR 10

GREEN STEW

Place a large pot over medium-high heat and toss in the butter. Swirl gently as the butter melts. As the water evaporates, tasty sediment will form and begin lightly browning toward golden and beyond. As soon as the bits are deliciously brown and nutty-smelling, stop the browning cold in its tracks by tossing in the garlic and a few splashes of the water. Sauté the garlic until it's softening but not browning, a minute or so. Pour in the remaining water. Toss in all the vegetables and sprinkle them with salt and pepper. Stir just enough to combine. Cover tightly and steam the works, stirring occasionally, until just tender, 3 or 4 minutes. Serve and share!

¼ cup (60 mL) of butter

4 garlic cloves, thinly sliced

½ cup (125 mL) of water

1 bunch of broccoli, broken into small florets

1 bunch of asparagus, tough bottoms trimmed away, stalks cut into 3 pieces

1 bunch of kale, trimmed and thinly sliced (or 8 cups/2 L baby spinach— about a 5-ounce/142 g bag)

2 cups (500 mL) of fresh or frozen green peas

2 cups (500 mL) of frozen green beans, or a big handful of fresh ones cut in half

1 teaspoon (5 mL) of salt

Lots of freshly ground pepper

FAMILY FLAVORS

Colors in vegetables mean nutrition, and cooking improves that nutrition. But don't overcook that color to dull and muted, or the vegetable loses its vitality. There's a tight connection between beautiful color and peak nutrition. The better and brighter the color looks, the better the veg is for you. Cook from pale raw green to bright cooked green, but not on to dull, overcooked green.

THIS TIMELESS GROUP OF FLAVORS IS A DEEPLY SATISFYING WAY TO PUT A POWERFUL punch of vegetables on the table packed with bright, sunny flavor. This version of classic ratatouille adds the fix-it-and-forget-it ease of roasting, with a finishing flourish of fresh basil. SERVES 4

BASIL RATATOUILLE

2 zucchini

1 eggplant

2 red bell peppers

1 red onion

1 pint (500 mL) of cherry
    tomatoes, halved

Cloves from 1 head of garlic, halved

¼ cup (60 mL) of olive oil

1 teaspoon (5 mL) of salt

Lots of freshly ground pepper

Leaves from 2 bunches of fresh
    basil, torn

Preheat your oven to 425°F (220°C). Turn on your convection fan if you have one.

Evenly quarter the zucchini lengthwise, then evenly cube it further. Evenly cube the eggplant, bell peppers and onion, using this cut size as your guide.

Toss the zucchini, bell peppers, onion, cherry tomatoes and garlic with the olive oil, salt and pepper. Add the eggplant (any earlier and it unevenly absorbs the oil) and toss again. Spread the vegetables in a baking dish or roasting pan.

Roast for 1 hour or so, giving them a quick stir after 30 minutes and again after 45 minutes. Feel free to serve immediately or turn off the oven and leave for later. Either way, when ready to serve and share, scatter the basil over the works.

FAMILY FLAVORS

As my family sits down to enjoy ratatouille, we think of the families where this dish originates and how many healthy vegetables they eat. This classic dish is simply that: a way for the gardeners and cooks of Provence and all along the sunny shore of the Mediterranean to gather, prepare and share their bounty with their families.

YOU DON'T NEED AN EXCUSE TO EAT KALE. IT'S PACKED WITH ENOUGH INTENSE nutrition and deep flavor to hook you all by itself. But if you *did* need an excuse, bacon is probably the best one. Actually, here's a better story: The bacon isn't for you, it's for the kale. Maybe because kale is so darn good, it deserves a little bacon love now and then! SERVES 4 TO 6

BACON KALE

Toss the bacon into a soup pot. Add ¼ cup (60 mL) of water (this helps the bacon cook evenly). Set the heat to medium-high and cook, stirring often, until the water is evaporated and the bacon is crisp, 10 minutes or so.

Meanwhile, strip out the stems of the kale, holding down each folded leaf with one hand and pulling the stem away with the other. Slice the stems as thinly as possible and cut the leaves into 6 or 8 pieces each.

When the bacon is crisp, pour off half or so of the tasty fat, reluctantly letting it go for the greater good. Splash in another ¼ cup (60 mL) water—stand back, because it splatters—and stir a moment to clean up the pan. When the water simmers, toss in the kale stems. When the water returns to a simmer, cram in the kale leaves. Cover tightly and steam the kale until tender, 3 or 4 minutes. Stir, serve and share!

4 slices of bacon, diced

1 large bunch of kale (or 2 smaller ones)

FAMILY FLAVORS

It's not about the bacon. It's about the kale. The bacon is just along for the ride. An afterthought, really. That's your story. Stick to it or you'll blow your vegetable cover story!

THIS IS MY FAVORITE WAY TO COOK BARLEY. BARLEY ON ITS OWN CAN BE A TOUCH boring, but stir in some nutty butter, nutty squash and aromatic thyme, and this healthy whole grain will light up the plate. This is a hearty side dish for warming up a cold day. It's full of nutrition and packed with flavor. SERVES 6 AS A SIDE

BAKED BUTTERNUT BARLEY

2 tablespoons (30 mL) of butter

1 onion, chopped

4 garlic cloves, thinly sliced

1 butternut squash, peeled, halved
   lengthwise, seeded and diced

1 cup (250 mL) of any barley

4 cups (1 L) of water

½ teaspoon (2 mL) of salt

Freshly ground pepper

Leaves from a few sprigs of fresh
   thyme or sage, chopped (or
   1 teaspoon/5 mL dried)

Preheat your oven to 325°F (160°C).

Toss the butter into a medium ovenproof saucepan over medium-high heat. Swirl gently as the butter melts. As the water evaporates, tasty sediment will form and begin lightly browning toward golden and beyond. As soon as the bits are deliciously brown and nutty-smelling, stop the browning cold in its tracks by tossing in the onions and garlic. Cook as the vegetables heat through and their flavors brighten, 2 or 3 minutes.

Add the squash and stir, heating it through, softening it slightly and lightly coloring the works, 4 or 5 minutes. Add the barley, pour in the water and sprinkle in the salt and pepper. Bring to a furious boil, then reduce the heat to a slow, steady simmer. Cover tightly and place in your oven.

Bake until the barley and squash are tender and flavorful and the water is absorbed, 45 minutes. If the barley seems watery, continue baking for another 10 minutes or so. Just before serving and sharing, stir in the thyme.

FAMILY FLAVORS

You'll enjoy a powerful feeling of well-earned accomplishment when you watch your table shoveling down loads of whole grains. This dish is so delicious that you'll all forget how healthy it is as you empty your bowls. Life's little miracles!

WHEAT BERRIES—WHOLE WHEAT KERNELS—ARE THE WHOLEST OF THE WHOLE grains, each little kernel a full grain of wheat. The flours we derive from grains are a huge part of today's diet, but they're often so refined that they lose the vitality of the whole form. Wheat berries take a while to cook, but your reward will be chewy yet tender, healthy and delicious. MAKES 3 CUPS (750 ML)

ROSEMARY WHEAT BERRIES

Preheat your oven to 325°F (160°C).

Toss the butter into a medium ovenproof saucepan over medium-high heat. Add the onions, carrot, celery and garlic and cook, stirring frequently, just long enough for them to sizzle, soften and lightly brown, 2 or 3 minutes or so.

Pour in the water and sprinkle in the salt. Stir in the wheat berries, bay leaf and rosemary. Bring to a furious boil, then cover tightly and place in the oven. Bake until the wheat berries are tender but chewy, 90 minutes or so. (Alternatively, pour in an extra 1 cup/250 mL of water and simmer, covered, for 90 minutes.) If the wheat berries have a bit more moisture than you'd like, simply stir over high heat for a few moments as they dry out a bit. Stir in the green onions, serve and share!

1 tablespoon (15 mL) of butter
1 or 2 onions, chopped
1 carrot, chopped
1 celery rib, chopped
1 or 2 garlic cloves, minced
3 cups (750 mL) of water
1 teaspoon (5 mL) of sea salt
1 cup (250 mL) of wheat berries
1 bay leaf
Leaves from 1 sprig of fresh rosemary, minced (or 1 teaspoon/5 mL dried)
2 green onions, thinly sliced

FAMILY FLAVORS
- - - - - - - - - - - -
If anything, this dish is the opposite of gluten-free, but for some of us gluten intolerance is very real. Recognize that whatever challenges we may face, the single most important contribution you can make to your family's health is cooking real food every day.

THE BRILLIANT DEEP RED OF BEETS IS A SIGN OF THEIR NUTRITIONAL MIGHT AND BIG, bright flavor. Stir in quinoa and you're into the deep end of healthy flavor! MAKES ABOUT 4 CUPS (1 L)

BEET-RED QUINOA

1 large or 2 small beets, peeled,
  grated through the large holes
  of a box grater
2 cups (500 mL) of water
1 cup (250 mL) of quinoa, well rinsed
1 tablespoon (15 mL) of olive oil
1 tablespoon (15 mL) of honey
½ teaspoon (2 mL) of salt
1 teaspoon (5 mL) of red wine vinegar

Toss the beets into a small pot. Pour in the water and add the quinoa, olive oil, honey and salt. Bring to a furious boil, then reduce the heat to the slowest, steadiest simmer possible. You may find that even your lowest heat is still too much, so try offsetting your pot a bit from the heat. Cover and gently simmer until the quinoa is brilliant red and tender, 15 minutes or so. Turn off the heat but don't uncover the works, and let rest for 5 minutes. Unveil and stir in the vinegar. Serve and share!

FAMILY FLAVORS
- - - - - - - - - - - -
In nature the color intensity of a vegetable is a sign of its nutritional vitality. Because beets are bright red, they're packed with micronutrients—and flavor. Healthful or not, their red juice can stain your fingers, so consider lightly oiling your hands or slipping on a pair of disposable gloves to minimize the mess.

A GOOD OLD-FASHIONED HODGEPODGE IS THE FASTEST AND SIMPLEST WAY TO COOK hard, soft and green vegetables together, efficiently harnessing a pot, water and heat to get dinner on the table in a hurry. You can stew vegetables with just as much passion and flame as any meat-themed stew. Here's how. SERVES 4 TO 6, WITH LEFTOVERS, MAYBE

GARDEN HODGEPODGE

Place a large, heavy pot over medium-high heat. Toss in the butter, swirling, sizzling and lightly browning. Stir in the aromatic onions, celery and garlic, sautéing and softening, 3 or 4 minutes.

Add the harder vegetables—the potatoes and carrots. Pour in the water and season with salt and pepper. Give the works a good stir and bring to a good simmer. Cover tightly and simmer furiously, stirring often and vigorously, until the hard vegetables are soft enough to enjoy in your bowl, 15 minutes or so.

Stir in the thyme, green beans and chard. Splash in a few tablespoons of water, cover, lower the heat a bit and steam gently for 3 or 4 minutes. Stir, serve and share!

¼ cup (60 mL) of butter

2 onions, minced

2 celery ribs, sliced

4 garlic cloves, thinly sliced

2 large or 3 or 4 smaller potatoes, cut into big bite-size pieces

2 carrots, sliced ½ inch (1 cm) thick

2 cups (500 mL) of water

1 teaspoon (5 mL) of salt

Lots of freshly ground pepper

A big handful of minced fresh thyme

A few handfuls of yellow or green beans, tougher tips removed, cut into 2 or 3 shorter pieces

A big bunch or two of chard, kale or spinach, trimmed and chopped

FAMILY FLAVORS

Much of what we know as cooking was developed all over the real world where speed and convenience are prized. So often that simplicity shows the true path. Follow it for flavor.

I GET A JOLT OUT OF JUST LOOKING AT SWEET POTATOES, KNOWING HOW NUTRITIOUS they are. So of all the ways I know how to cook a sweet potato, when I cook them this way, you know I get really excited. Try them and see how you feel. You're welcome! SERVES 4

CHILI-GLAZED SWEET POTATOES

2 large sweet potatoes

2 tablespoons (30 mL) of red
  pepper jelly

1 tablespoon (15 mL) of cumin seeds

1 teaspoon (5 mL) of coriander seeds

1 teaspoon (5 mL) of your favorite
  hot sauce

½ teaspoon (2 mL) of salt

Preheat your oven to 400°F (200°C). Get out a medium baking pan.

Cut each sweet potato in half lengthwise. Use the sharp point of a small knife to score the flesh, ½ inch (1 cm) deep at ½ inch (1 cm) intervals. Position the potatoes cut side up in your baking pan and bake for 45 minutes.

Meanwhile, spoon the jelly into a small bowl and stir in the cumin seeds, coriander seeds, hot sauce and salt until well combined. Evenly spoon and smear the glaze all over the cut surface of the oven-hot potatoes. Continue to bake until the sweet potatoes are glazed and tender, another 15 minutes. Serve and share!

FAMILY FLAVORS

This scoring/seasoning/baking/
glazing method is my homage
to the sweet potato because it's
of course super-healthy but also
simultaneously wildly flavorful
and all-dressed-up beautiful. It's
a good day to be a sweet potato!

SOME FLAVORS GO TOGETHER NATURALLY. THEY ARE JUST PLAIN DELICIOUS together no matter how you cook them. This dish is full of such harmonies. The roasting adds yet another dimension of deliciousness. SERVES 4 TO 6

CURRY ROAST SWEET POTATOES WITH SOUR APPLES

Preheat your oven to 350°F (180°C). Turn on your convection fan if you have one.

Cut the sweet potatoes and apples into pieces roughly equal in size. Big chunks or cubes are fine, but if you like, take the time to produce a pile of precise dice for a bit of finesse. This dish is delicious either way.

Toss the sweet potatoes and apples into a large bowl. Splash in the oil and sprinkle in the cumin seeds, fennel seeds, coriander seeds, curry powder, salt and pepper. Toss the works together, evenly mixing the flavors, textures and colors. Spread out in a baking dish or roasting pan and roast as the flavors deepen and textures soften, 1 hour or so. Serve and share!

2 large sweet potatoes (unpeeled)

6 big crisp apples (unpeeled), cored

¼ cup (60 mL) of olive oil

1 heaping tablespoon (20 mL) of cumin seeds

1 heaping tablespoon (20 mL) of fennel seeds

1 heaping tablespoon (20 mL) of coriander seeds

1 heaping tablespoon (20 mL) of curry powder

½ teaspoon (20 mL) of salt

Lots of freshly ground pepper

FAMILY FLAVORS

When you're the CEO of a busy family operation, key facts and figures matter. So you'll want to know that sweet potatoes are the most nutritionally dense vegetable in the kitchen. You don't have to remember everything, just the important stuff. Like figuring out every possible way you can cook these gems for your family at least once a week!

SWEETS
& TREATS

FAMILY RECIPES

THIS ONE'S FUN. YOU CAN WHIP UP THESE PUDDINGS IN ADVANCE, THEN WHEN IT'S time to serve them, set up a mini whipped cream station and invite the kids—big or small—to invent their own flavored topping. SERVES 6 TO 8

YOUR CHOCOLATE COCONUT PUDDING AND YOUR KIDS' WHIPPED CREAM

FOR THE PUDDING

12 ounces (340 g) of bittersweet
  dark chocolate

2 cans (14 ounces/400 mL each)
  of coconut milk

¼ cup (60 mL) of brown sugar
  or molasses

1 teaspoon (5 mL) of ground allspice
  (for optional mysterious flavor)

2 shots of spiced rum if the kids
  aren't around

1 tablespoon (15 mL) of pure
  vanilla extract

FOR THE WHIPPED CREAM

1 cup (250 mL) of whipping cream,
  chilled

1 tablespoon (15 mL) of any sugar,
  honey or molasses (or ¼ cup/
  60 mL of your favorite jam, jelly
  or marmalade)

1 tablespoon (15 mL) of pure
  vanilla extract

A shot of your favorite booze
  if the spirit moves you

Chop the chocolate into smallish chunks and chuck into a medium bowl. In a small saucepan, bring the coconut milk, brown sugar and allspice to a furious boil, then immediately pour over the chopped chocolate. Splash in the rum and vanilla. Whisk slowly until the chocolate is melted and smooth. Divide the pudding among your chosen vessels, cover the surface with plastic wrap, and chill until firm, at least an hour. Meanwhile, freeze a medium bowl.

When you're ready to serve, ready Operation Whipped Cream. Measure the cream into the frozen bowl and follow with your choice of sweeteners and flavorings. Whisk the works vigorously until firm, creamy peaks form, 3 to 5 minutes by hand, less with a mixer. Top the puddings, grab your spoons, serve and share!

FAMILY FLAVORS

Mason jars often come in handy in a busy kitchen. I particularly like how easy it is to half-fill a wide-mouth half-pint (250 mL) jar with this pudding, screw on the lid and fit into the nooks and crannies of a crammed-full refrigerator. They have exactly enough room left in them for the proceeds of Operation Whipped Cream.

IF YOU'RE CRAVING THE DEEP, RICH FLAVOR OF A FRESHLY BAKED CHOCOLATE CAKE, try baking a round of mini cakes instead of one great big one. You actually want these little flourless wonders to collapse, because when they do, they make lots of room for whipped cream! MAKES 12 MINI TREATS

FALLEN CHOCOLATE CAKE STUFFED WITH WHIPPED CREAM

Preheat your oven to 400°F (200°C). Turn on your convection fan if you have one. Lightly butter a muffin pan and dust each muffin cup with sugar, tapping out the excess.

Toss the chocolate and butter into a large bowl set over a slightly smaller pot of simmering water. Stir until the chocolate is almost melted, then remove from the heat and whisk until smooth.

In a medium bowl, whisk together the eggs, sugar, cocoa powder and vanilla until well combined. Whisk the egg mixture into the chocolate until smooth. Divide the batter evenly among the prepared muffin cups. Bake for 10 minutes. Transfer pan to a rack. As the cakes cool, their centers will cave in.

While the cakes bake, whisk together the whipping cream, sugar and vanilla until firm, creamy peaks form, 3 to 5 minutes by hand, less with a mixer.

When the cakes are cool enough to handle, turn them out of the pan. Top with spoonfuls of whipped cream. Serve and share!

FOR THE FALLEN CHOCOLATE CAKE

8 ounces (225 g) of bittersweet dark
   chocolate, chopped
½ cup (125 mL) of butter
4 eggs
½ cup (125 mL) of white sugar
2 tablespoons (30 mL) of
   cocoa powder
1 tablespoon (15 mL) of pure
   vanilla extract

FOR THE WHIPPED CREAM

2 cups (500 mL) of whipping
   cream, chilled
2 tablespoons (30 mL) of brown sugar
1 tablespoon (15 mL) of pure
   vanilla extract

FAMILY FLAVORS

These treats are the sort of bribe you hold on to until you really need something done. You can empty and clean an entire garage with the promise of a batch. Watch lawns get mowed and snowy walks be shoveled as you float the promise of these delicious little cakes. An army marches on its stomach!

IT'S EASY IN LIFE AND THE KITCHEN TO CONFUSE THE UNFAMILIAR WITH THE DIFFICULT. Do you think Italian cooks like being stuck in the kitchen any more than we do? You won't believe how easy it is to pull off this dessert. Get ready to impress yourself in your own kitchen. SERVES 8 OR 9

GINGERSNAP TIRAMISU

1 cup (250 mL) of rich mascarpone
   cheese

¼ cup (60 mL) of brown sugar

¼ cup (60 mL) of amaretto or
   Frangelico liqueur

2 cups (500 mL) of whipping cream

A 425 g (1 lb) package of Kookie
   Kutter Ginger Snaps or other thin
   rectangular cookies

1 cup (250 mL) of strong coffee
   or espresso

1 cup (250 mL) or so of coarsely
   grated bittersweet dark chocolate

Spoon the mascarpone into a large bowl. Measure in the sugar and splash in the amaretto. Whisk together evenly. Pour in the cream and whisk the works vigorously until firm, creamy peaks form, 3 to 5 minutes by hand, less with a mixer. Set aside.

One by one, dip the gingersnaps into the coffee, immersing fully for a moment before evenly arranging in an 8-inch (2 L) square baking dish. Use half the gingersnaps, forming 2 thin layers. Evenly spread a thick layer of half the mascarpone mixture over the cookies. Top with half of the grated chocolate. Make 1 more layer in the same manner. Cover and chill until it firm, at least 2 hours or overnight. Scoop, serve, share and take a bow!

> **FAMILY FLAVORS**
> - - - - - - - - - -
> If you can't find Kookie Kutter Ginger Snaps at your grocery store, substitute ladyfingers or other rectangular cookies that will fit into your pan. Don't use round gingersnaps. Form and function!

THINK OF THIS AS A WEEKEND PROJECT. FIND SOMEONE TO SHARE THE FUN WITH, set aside some time together and get baking. All the defining elements of a Boston cream pie are here, just in cupcake form. The separate parts are easy to assemble, and there are batter spoons to lick and leftover chocolate to paint on noses too! MAKES 12 STUFFED CUPCAKES

BOSTON CREAM CUPCAKES

Preheat your oven to 350°F (180°C). Turn on your convection fan if you have one. Lightly butter a muffin pan and dust each muffin cup with sugar, tapping out the excess.

Start with the cupcakes. In a medium bowl, whisk together the flour, nutmeg, baking powder and salt. Crack the eggs into the bowl of your stand mixer and measure in the sugar, honey and vanilla. Beat on high speed, scraping down the sides of the bowl occasionally, until thick, smooth and frothy. Meanwhile, heat the milk and butter together in a small saucepan just long enough to melt the butter, not long enough to simmer.

Sprinkle the flour mixture into the frothy egg. Stir slowly, just enough to evenly combine everything. With the mixer on low speed, slowly pour a stream of the hot milk into the works. Mix just until combined.

Divide the batter among the muffin cups and bake until golden, firm and tender, 20 minutes or so. Let rest on a rack until cool enough to handle, then carefully turn out onto a baking sheet and cool completely.

Now make the white chocolate cream. Measure the cream, sugar, cornstarch and vanilla into a small saucepan. Heat gently, stirring often, until the mixture thickens, just 2 or 3 minutes. Immediately remove from the heat and toss in the chocolate. Stir until melted and smooth. Cool to room temperature before using, or cover and refrigerate for longer.

To make the frosting, in a small saucepan, bring the cream to a furious boil, then immediately remove from the heat and toss in the chocolate. Stir until melted and smooth. Cool to room temperature before using, or cover and refrigerate for longer (in which case, bring it back to room temperature before using).

To assemble the cupcakes, using a serrated knife, carefully cut the crown off each cupcake, just below its top edge. Set the tops aside. Carefully spoon out a hollow, about 1 inch (2.5 cm) deep. Have a snack with the pickings—baker's privilege. Evenly fill the hollows with the white chocolate cream, spreading any extra on top. Cap each cupcake with its mate. Evenly spoon the chocolate frosting over the works while you battle off the scavengers. Serve and share!

FOR THE NUTMEG VANILLA CUPCAKES

2½ cups (625 mL) of all-purpose flour

1 tablespoon (15 mL) of nutmeg

2 teaspoons (10 mL) of baking powder

½ teaspoon (2 mL) of salt

4 eggs

1 cup (250 mL) of white sugar

2 tablespoons (30 mL) of honey

1 tablespoon (15 mL) of pure
   vanilla extract

1 cup (250 mL) of milk

½ cup (125 mL) of butter

FOR THE WHITE CHOCOLATE CREAM

2 cups (500 mL) of whipping cream

½ cup (125 mL) of white sugar

¼ cup (60 mL) of cornstarch

1 tablespoon (15 mL) of pure
   vanilla extract

8 ounces (225 g) of white chocolate,
   chopped

FOR THE DARK CHOCOLATE FROSTING

½ cup (125 mL) of whipping cream

4 ounces (115 g) of bittersweet dark
   chocolate, chopped

THESE SQUARES ARE REALLY JUST COOKIES IN A DIFFERENT FORM. THE FLAVORS and method are similar. This is an excellent treat to show off caramel chips, but feel free to skip straight to chocolate chips or experiment with other candies in the batter. MAKES 12 TO 16 TREATS

CARAMEL CHIP BLONDIES

1 cup (250 mL) of butter,
　at room temperature
1 cup (250 mL) of brown sugar
1 cup (250 mL) of white sugar
2 eggs
1 tablespoon (15 mL) of pure
　vanilla extract
2 cups (500 mL) of all-purpose flour
2 cups (500 mL) of caramel chips
　or your favorite candy bits, divided
　in half

Preheat your oven to 350°F (180°C). Turn on your convection fan if you have one. Line a 13- × 9-inch (3.5 L) cake pan with parchment paper, extending the paper over the long sides to act as handles. Lightly spray the paper with cooking spray.

Toss the butter into the bowl of your stand mixer. Measure in the brown and white sugar. Beat on high speed until thick and smooth, scraping down the sides now and then. Add the eggs and vanilla, then beat until thick and creamy. Add the flour. Stir on low speed just until combined. Too much mixing will toughen the bars. Stir in half the caramel chips.

With a lightly oiled spatula, carefully spread the batter into the cake pan, smoothing the top. Sprinkle evenly with the remaining chips. Bake until firm, lightly browned and aromatic, 30 to 40 minutes. Cool completely in the pan. Using the paper handles, carefully lift the blondies from the pan. Cut as you wish, serve and share!

FAMILY FLAVORS

Kids deserve treats now and then, even daily after the veggies are gone. For maximum effect and fun, get your kids involved in baking these blondies. Somehow it feels so much better as a parent when you take the time to make them from scratch and turn it into a family project. And it's not junk food if it's homemade!

WHY NOT DO A LITTLE TREAT-BAKING FOR YOUR FAMILY? WHY WOULDN'T YOU indulge your chocolate cravings? Why wouldn't you stir chocolate chips into brownies? Why let factories cook for you? A lot to ponder, but no worries. All will be answered with the first bite! MAKES 12 LARGE OR 16 MEDIUM TREATS

CHOCOLATE CHIP BROWNIES

Preheat your oven to 350°F (180°C). Turn on your convection fan if you have one. Line a 13- × 9-inch (3.5 L) cake pan with parchment paper, extending the paper over the long sides to act as handles. Lightly spray the paper with cooking spray.

Toss the chocolate and butter into a medium bowl set over a slightly smaller pot of simmering water. Stir until melted and smooth, then remove from the heat.

In another medium bowl, whisk together the flour, cocoa powder, baking powder and salt.

Crack the eggs into the bowl of your stand mixer. Measure in the sugar and vanilla. Beat on high speed until thick, creamy and smooth, scraping down the sides now and then. Smoothly stir in the melted chocolate mixture. Add the flour and stir on low speed just until evenly mixed. Too much mixing will toughen the brownies. Stir in half of the chocolate chips.

With a lightly oiled spatula, carefully spread the batter into the cake pan, smoothing the top. Sprinkle evenly with the remaining chips. Bake for 30 to 35 minutes. Cool completely in the pan. Using the paper handles, carefully lift the brownies from the pan. Cut as you wish, serve and share!

1 pound (450 g) of bittersweet dark chocolate, chopped

1 cup (250 mL) of butter

2 cups (500 mL) of all-purpose flour

½ cup (125 mL) of cocoa powder

1 teaspoon (5 mL) of baking powder

½ teaspoon (2 mL) of salt

4 eggs

2 cups (500 mL) of white or brown sugar

2 tablespoons (30 mL) of pure vanilla extract

2 cups (500 mL) of chocolate chips or your favorite chocolate candy bits, divided in half

FAMILY FLAVORS

This brownie batter is bomb-proof, so it's a good recipe for any novice bakers in your family. Even if they mix up a few details, with this much chocolate the results are always delicious!

An easy batch of brownies up your sleeve comes in handy. Lunchboxes, treat tables, bake sales, get-well gifts, party favors, long-delayed return of borrowed gear, outright bribes. Everybody loves a good brownie!

THESE COOKIES ARE DELICIOUS, AND SINCE IT'S JUST AS EASY TO MAKE A LOT AS A little, this is a big recipe. After one bite you'll understand why. You'll want lots to share and a few to hoard for yourself. MAKES ABOUT 3 DOZEN BIG COOKIES

CINNAMON OATMEAL COOKIES

5 cups (1.25 L) of quick-cooking
  rolled oats
3 cups (750 mL) of all-purpose flour
1 tablespoon (15 mL) of baking powder
1 teaspoon (5 mL) of salt
1 pound (450 g) of butter, at room
  temperature
3 cups (750 mL) of brown sugar
1 tablespoon (15 mL) of cinnamon
1 tablespoon (15 mL) of pure
  vanilla extract
2 eggs

Preheat your oven to 350°F (180°C). Turn on your convection fan if you have one. Adjust your shelves so 2 trays can bake evenly at once. Line 2 or 3 cookie sheets with parchment paper or nonstick baking mats.

In a medium bowl, whisk together the oats, flour, baking powder and salt.

Toss the butter into the bowl of your stand mixer. Measure in the sugar, cinnamon and vanilla. Beat on high speed until thick and smooth, scraping down the sides now and then. Add the eggs and beat until thick and creamy. Add the oat mixture and beat on slow speed just until evenly mixed. Too much mixing will toughen the cookies.

Use a ¼-cup (60 mL) measure to evenly portion the cookie dough. With your fingers, roll each portion into a ball. Place about 8 balls evenly on each cookie sheet and press down gently until their diameter doubles. Smooth the tops and edges with your fingers.

Bake in batches until the cookies have slumped and spread, firmed up and lightly browned, 15 minutes or so. Cool on racks. Repeat with the remaining dough. Beat back the zombie mob. Serve and share!

FAMILY FLAVORS

These cookies are tender and chewy, but their secret is the boldness of their flavor. No tentative sprinkle of cinnamon or drops of vanilla here. It takes big spoonfuls of flavor to compete with Big Food Inc.'s factory flavors.

This cookie recipe is perfect for any aspiring bakers in your midst to flex their skills. They may make a mess, but they'll also make a memory and just might get hooked on baking!

WHAT A TREAT! AND SO EASY TO MAKE FOR A CROWD WHEN YOU MAKE THE cookies ahead and have them ready to go in the freezer. Want it even easier? Freeze the finished sandwiches ahead! MAKES 20 TREATS FOR A BIRTHDAY PARTY

ICE CREAM SANDWICHES

Preheat your oven to 350°F (180°F). Turn on your convection fan if you have one. Adjust your shelves so 2 trays can bake evenly at once. Line 2 or 3 cookie sheets with parchment paper or nonstick baking mats.

In a medium bowl, whisk together the flour, cocoa powder, baking soda and salt.

Toss the butter into the bowl of your stand mixer. Measure in the white sugar, brown sugar and vanilla. Beat on high speed until thick and smooth, scraping down the sides now and then. Add the eggs and beat until thick and creamy. Add the flour mixture and beat on slow speed just until evenly mixed. Too much mixing will toughen the cookies.

Evenly scoop out the dough and with your hands roll into balls. Arrange 12 balls on each cookie sheet, leaving them lots of room to spread as they bake (they will double in size). Bake in batches until the cookies have slumped, flattened and firmed, 10 minutes or so. Transfer to racks to cool completely. Repeat with the remaining dough.

While the cookies bake, line a baking sheet with parchment paper. Scoop out ½ cup (125 mL) of ice cream and flatten between two smaller pieces of parchment to form an even puck-shaped disk about 1 inch (2.5 cm) thick. Place on the baking sheet and repeat with the remaining ice cream. Freeze until needed.

Build sandwiches with the ice cream. Serve, share and make more to fold in parchment and freeze for next time, or freeze the leftover cookies for future assembly.

2 cups (500 mL) of all-purpose flour

½ cup (125 mL) of cocoa powder

1 teaspoon (5 mL) of baking soda

½ teaspoon (2 mL) of salt

1 cup (250 mL) of butter, at
room temperature

1 cup (250 mL) of white sugar

1 cup (250 mL) of brown sugar

1 tablespoon (15 mL) of pure
vanilla extract

2 eggs

2½ quarts (2.5 L) of your favorite
ice cream

FAMILY FLAVORS

There are many reasons to love a round of these ice cream sandwiches. One of the best is how far in advance you can make them. Make them this week, eat them next week. You can conquer your busy schedule and gear up for a party well in advance. And anyway, these treats taste way better pre-frozen!

THIS RECIPE IS FOR ALL OF YOU WHO NEED A SIGNATURE PARTY TRICK. HAVING A dinner party? Trying to impress your kids? Leaping flames! Dangerous heat! Cooking on the edge! This showstopper is always a winner. SERVES 6 TO 8

FLAMING BANANA SPLITS

FOR THE CHOCOLATE SAUCE

2 cups (500 mL) of whipping cream

¼ cup (60 mL) of cocoa powder

¼ cup (60 mL) of brown sugar

1 tablespoon (15 mL) of pure
vanilla extract

4 ounces (115 g) of bittersweet dark
chocolate, chopped

2 tablespoons (30 mL) of rum

FOR THE STRAWBERRY SAUCE

2 cups (500 mL) of frozen strawberries

1 cup (250 mL) of strawberry jam

1 cup (250 mL) of orange juice

FOR THE CHOCOLATE WHIPPED CREAM

1 cup (250 mL) of whipping cream

2 tablespoons (30 mL) of
cocoa powder

1 tablespoon (15 mL) of white sugar

1 teaspoon (5 mL) of pure
vanilla extract

FOR THE FLAMING BANANAS

¼ cup (60 mL) of butter

½ cup (125 mL) of brown sugar

4 ripe bananas, halved lengthwise

¼ cup (60 mL) of dark spiced rum

FOR FINISH AND FLOURISH

Your favorite vanilla ice cream

Crunchy chocolate sprinkles

Crumbled vanilla wafers or the like

A few maraschino cherries

If you haven't flambéed before, practice beforehand, with a small amount of rum in your pan—without the sugar and bananas—so you'll know what to expect.

Make and chill the sauces first, even days in advance. First, the chocolate sauce. In a small saucepan, measure the cream, cocoa powder, sugar and vanilla. Whisking constantly over medium heat, bring to a slow, steady simmer. Remove from the heat, add the chocolate and stir until melted and smooth. Stir in the rum, then pour into a jar and chill.

Next, the strawberry sauce. Toss the strawberries, jam and juice into a small saucepan. Stirring steadily over medium heat, bring to a slow, steady simmer. Remove from the heat and carefully purée the works as smooth as silk with a hand blender. Pour into a jar and chill.

When you're ready for the show, ready the cream. Vigorously whisk the cream, cocoa powder, sugar and vanilla until firm, creamy peaks form, 3 to 5 minutes by hand, less with a mixer. Chill.

Now, here's how to safely flambé a pan of bananas and light a party on fire without an insurance claim. Roll up your sleeves and tie your hair back if it's long. Turn off your exhaust fan. Have the pan's lid nearby just in case things get out of hand. Preheat your largest, heaviest skillet or sauté pan over medium-high heat. Toss in the butter. As soon as it begins to melt and sizzle, follow with the brown sugar. Swirl the pan gently as the sugar melts into the butter and begins bubbling here and there. Continue swirling the works for a moment or two, then lay in the bananas, swirling and tossing them in the pan to absorb the flavors. Rum up!

• IF YOU'RE USING A GAS STOVE, extend your arm, swing the sizzling pan away from the flame and tilt the far edge of the pan down and away from you. Pour the rum into the bottom corner with the bananas. Keeping your arm extended, tilt the edge of the pan toward the flame until the alcohol ignites.

• IF YOU'RE USING AN ELECTRIC STOVE, pour the rum over the bananas, shaking the pan to spread the alcohol around, and ignite by holding the edge of the pan near a lit candle.

Hold steadily as flame and applause erupt. Sauté as the flames die down, a minute or so longer, shaking and shivering (the pan, not you!). Assemble the banana splits any way you care to, because at this point you're the undisputed kitchen boss! Serve and share!

THIS RECIPE IS FOR YOUR KIDS TO HELP MAKE, ALTHOUGH THEIR JAWS WILL DROP IF you surprise them with it. Actually, even if they do help you make it, their jaws will still drop. Best ten bucks you'll ever spend. Give yourself lots of time—even a couple of days—for the chilling. SERVES 6 TO 8

STAINED GLASS JELLY

For the mosaic, lightly oil 4 or 5 plastic sandwich containers. Pour 1 cup (250 mL) of boiling water into each container. Stir a different color of jelly powder into each container until dissolved, ignoring the directions on the package and thereby doubling the strength. Cover and refrigerate until firm, a few hours or overnight.

Lightly oil an 8-inch (2 L) square cake pan. Without removing the set jelly from the containers, carefully cut it into even cubes. Using your fingers, carefully pry out the cubes and spread them evenly in the cake pan, gently mixing the colors.

For the frame, pour the cold water into a medium bowl and evenly sprinkle the gelatin over the surface. Rest as the gelatin dissolves and blooms, 5 minutes or so. Pour in the boiling water and stir until the gelatin melts. You'll know it's ready when you can't feel any grit between your fingers. Whisk in the condensed milk. Pour over the colors. Lightly stir with your fingers to evenly combine and settle the works. Refrigerate until firm, several hours, even overnight if you have the patience. Serve and share!

FOR THE COLORFUL CUBE MOSAIC

4 or 5 cups (1 or 1.25 L) of boiling water

4 or 5 packages (3 ounces/85 g each) of different-colored jelly powders (red, blue, purple, yellow, orange, green)

FOR THE FLAVORFUL WHITE FRAME

½ cup (125 mL) of cold water

2 envelopes (¼ ounce/7 g each) of unflavored gelatin

½ cup (125 mL) of boiling water

A 12-ounce (300 mL) can of sweetened condensed milk

FAMILY FLAVORS
- - - - - - - - - - - -
This dish is nothing but fun. It's loaded with sugar and not particularly redeeming other than for two powerful reasons: kids love how it tastes and it looks great. Sometimes that's enough, though, and it really adds to the fun if the kids help you make it. Even if they won't help the first time, they'll be lining up the second!

SPECIAL THANKS

I AM BLESSED TO LIVE WITHIN A CARING COMmunity, to be surrounded by a passionate team, and most important, to be a part of a loving family. I am reminded daily how fortunate we all are, and for that I am truly thankful.

Thank you, Prince Edward Island and all who make this such a special place to live, work, love and eat.

Thank you, Culinart Limited. Maureen, Edna, Vanessa, Anne and Stephanie, I couldn't do it without you. We work for each other.

Thank you, Chazz, for being more than my wife. You're an amazing partner, friend and inspiration and you bake a helluva chocolate cake!

And thank you, Gabe, Ariella and Camille. You inspire all of us to be our best and remind us every day what life is all about.

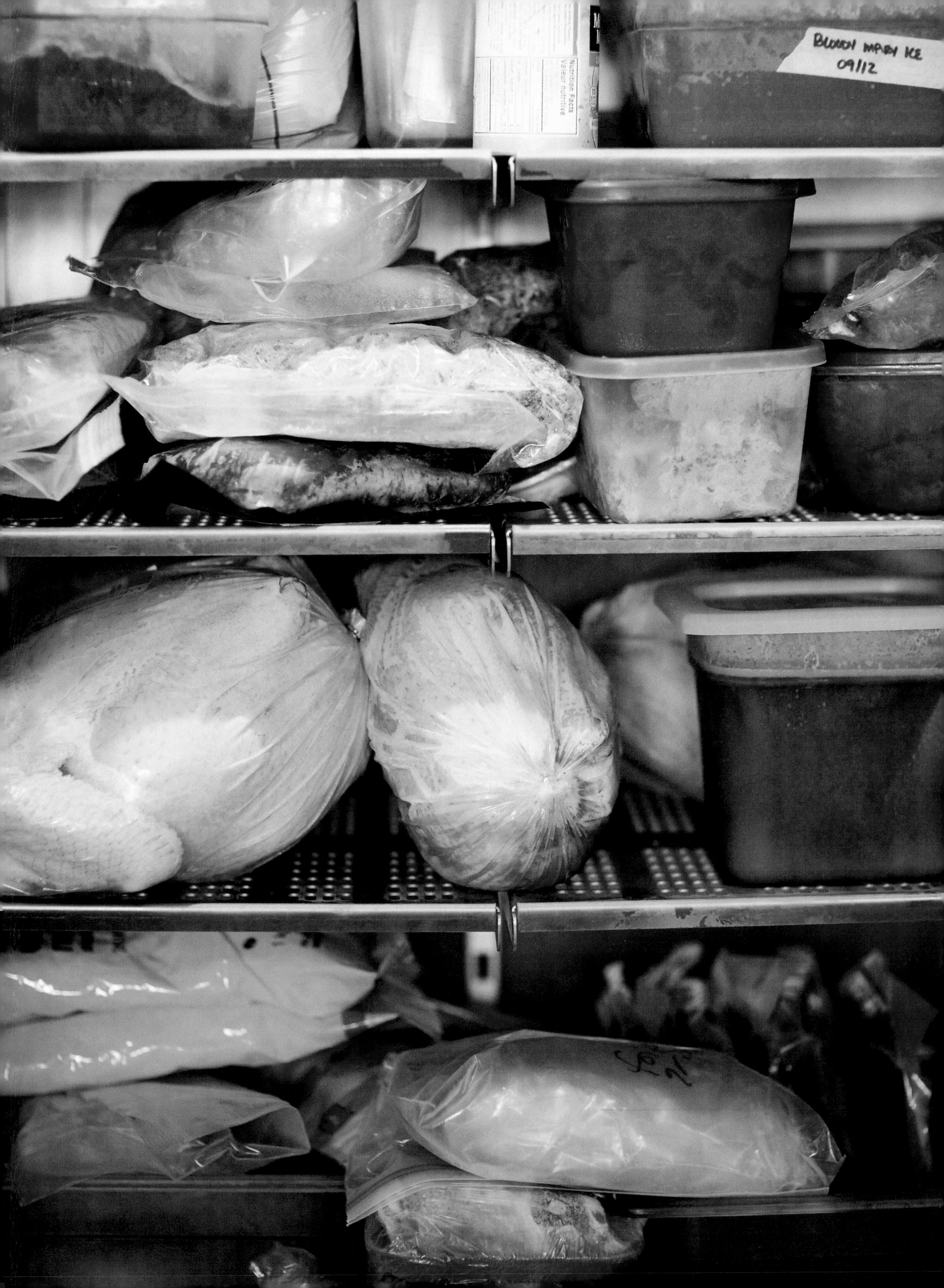
Nutrition Facts
Valeur nutritive
09/12

INDEX

34

36

38

44

46

48

50

52

54

SIMPLE
SALADS

58

60

62

COOK AHEAD